SAGE NEVADA

Nevada Spending and Government Efficiency (SAGE) Commission

Bipartisan Directions For Nevada's Future

by Frank Partlow

Table of Contents

Preface *by Phil Satre*

Frank Partlow is provocative, outspoken and seriously opinionated. He and I come from very different lifetime experiences – and wholly different political perspectives and parties. Conventional wisdom would suggest that there is little, if anything, that we could agree on that is important.

Nothing could be further from the truth.

We agree on a whole host of things that are fundamentally and urgently important to the future of Nevada – and are chronicled by Frank succinctly in *SAGE Nevada*. On the broadest basis, we agree:

That this State's future is in serious jeopardy and that something must be done – and soon

That the SAGE Commission report represents a credible, bipartisan effort by a group of dedicated and selfless Nevadans to tackle daunting economic realities that are not going to measurably change in the foreseeable future – and that will never be back to where they were prior to the Great Recession

That we cannot now, more than any period in recent history, wait for things to get better – we must change the way we spend taxpayers money in state government and we must become more efficient

We are running out of time – and money.

For eighteen months, 14 respected Nevadans from both parties and both ends of the State, volunteered their time to examine, dissect and analyze spending within the Executive Branch of state government and look for opportunities to increase efficiency under the auspices of the Nevada Spending and Government Efficiency (SAGE) Commission. Their final report was submitted to the governor January 7, 2010. *SAGE Nevada* is the story of that commission as told by Frank Partlow, who served as the Executive Director for SAGE.

Every concerned Nevada voter should be reading *SAGE Nevada*. I'm confident that voters, informed by this book, will overcome the stubborn resistance to change that favors the status quo and insist that we address the SAGE Commission's recommendations.

Likewise, each and every one of our 63 State Legislators in Nevada should read *SAGE Nevada* and own up to their responsibility for this State's future. It will be hard work, but it is too important to pass on to the next session. Don't let the SAGE report become one more commission report that gathers dust. We can't afford it.

Introduction *by Bruce R. James*

Frank Partlow captures the essence of the inner-workings of the Nevada SAGE Commission during its formation and its 18 months of work on behalf of the Governor and the Legislature to bring forward practical recommendations for streamlining our state government. With his long-time interest and involvement with the affairs of local governments he goes on to express his personal views on what needs to be done at both state and local levels to ensure that our tax dollars are well spent and that governments at all levels function smoothly for our citizens.

In the blunt language of an Army field-general, he wastes no words in pointing out the flaws that need to be fixed and offers many suggestions for doing so. In many ways this book is a field-manual for our elected officials and those aspiring to public service.

Frank has devoted most of his adult life to public service—from keeping us safe, to keeping governments running smoothly. As an Army officer it was his responsibility to implement the vision of the civilian leadership; the fact that he rose to become a Brigadier General shows that he was successful. We should all listen carefully when Frank says that our public employees can't be successful in serving our needs without a clearly articulated vision from our political leaders. When he says the spending process is broken, we had better pay attention. When he says the relationship between the state and local governments needs fixing, he is speaking as a person experienced in managing complex organizations that can't fail us.

The SAGE Commissioners and staff want to see our recommendations carefully considered by the Governor and legislators and implemented as soon as possible. This book helps move us forward in the process.

Author's Note

What's in a name? SAGE, an acronym for Spending and Government Efficiency Commission, suggests a kind of "triple entendre." Sage advice is wise advice. Sage is a plant, which grows well in arid, alkaline plains, like those in Nevada. Sage is also a spice, which can enhance the flavor of meats and hopefully, debates about the costs of government in Nevada.

This Commission would never have happened without the vision, persistence and willingness to put his money where his mouth is of one person, Bruce James. The State of Nevada and all its citizens owe him a huge debt of gratitude, whether they know it or not.

However, this book is not about Bruce James. It is not a government report. It is an account of my 20 months as Commission Executive Director, helping volunteer Nevadans approve 44 recommendations sent to the Governor. It includes my analysis regarding the way ahead. My observations and my commentaries are provided from the perspective of the 18 years I have been active in Nevada public policy issues in various other capacities.

The SAGE Commission's work was studiously non-partisan and well informed. However, headlines, commentaries and articles about it were often ill informed, biased and careless with facts. This book attempts to set the record straight.

The words "spending" and "saving" are two sides of the same coin. The "S" in SAGE, could describe either one, but it does not stand for "waste." The media persisted in calling SAGE the "waste" commission. Approaching government employees looking for "waste" implicitly accuses them of dishonesty, incompetence, or both. SAGE staff and commissioners believed that rather than such employees, they needed to find outdated, dysfunctional systems in which competent employees were required to work. Findings confirmed this approach.

I wish to thank Suzanne Kilgore and Daryl Drake for their assistance in organizing, editing and preparing this material. However, I take full responsibility for the entire contents of this book.

Chapter 1

The Status Quo Is Unaffordable

Although pundits and presidents keep saying that the worst recession since the Great Depression is over, national unemployment is still ten percent. At the beginning of the second decade of the 21st Century, every state in the union except North Dakota is broke. Unlike the federal government, which prints new money and borrows from China and its own grandchildren, states have the obligation to balance their budgets. Many, including Nevada, have severe restrictions on borrowing money for any purpose.

The recession is clearly not over in Nevada. National bond rating agencies call Nevada's the worst recession of any state. Unemployment here is 13%, gaming revenue is down over 11% and taxable sales have dropped over 17%. Nevada's neighbor, California, still the seventh largest economy in the world, is practically bankrupt. Since tourists have paid Nevada's fiscal needs over the years through gaming and sales taxes, when California sneezes, Nevada catches a cold. Now, California has pneumonia.

Las Vegas provides 75% of Nevada gaming related taxes, which make up 60% of the state's General Fund revenues. Las Vegas gaming related taxes have suffered double-digit declines. Recovery in Las Vegas will follow the rest of the US, if and when consumers again feel comfortable with discretionary spending, which "stays in Las Vegas." Some experts think Las Vegas may never return to its former profitability. That certainly won't happen in time for the state to return to even its 2007 fiscal revenues by 2013. Nevada's economy and fiscal revenues are not going to grow their way out of the fiscal crisis caused by this recession for a much more basic reason, however: The status quo in Nevada's state and local governments is simply unsustainable, because the current systems for providing this level of government services in Nevada are unaffordable.

The New Year, 2010, finds Nevada's governor trying to decide whether to call a special session of the legislature to deal with what is already a $60 million hole in the state's current budget. Earlier in 2009, that same legislature voted, over that same governor's veto, to approve one of the largest tax increases in Nevada's history to balance that budget.

That legislature also approved a resolution to review proposals for broad-based taxes, which are fair and equitable. Nineteen Nevadans have been nominated to work with a contracted research firm to recommend changes to Nevada's tax code. This initiative is being undertaken while 49 of 50 US states, each with significantly different tax codes, are suffering fiscal crises similar to those in Nevada. As the internationally respected news magazine, *Economist*, concluded on December 12, 2009: *While politicians mull tax increases and service cuts, public sector workers continue to gobble up money. . .The crisis, however, at least illuminates a simple fact.* ***The status quo is unaffordable.***

Families and businesses across the country understand that when short of money, the first step is to examine expenses for possible elimination or reduction, before attempting to generate new revenues. For governments at all levels, that sort of evaluation is doubly important because they spend money levied in taxes from these same citizens and businesses, which are having to cut their expenses to make ends meet.

That's where the Nevada SAGE Commission comes in. The "what" commission? Even well informed Nevadans know little about this commission's work, which resulted in 44 recommendations to the governor totaling approximately $2 billion in potential savings in the cost of state government over five years. This book is designed to inform all Nevadans about this commission and its work.

It is especially designed to help any Nevadan who wants to participate in the political process, which will elect candidates across the state in 2010. These are the brave Nevadans who will have to deal with what currently appears to be a $3 billion hole in a 2011-2013 budget of $8 billion. Nevada's cities and counties like those across the country face similar fiscal challenges. Electioneering slogans like "no new taxes; it's for the kids, or lock up the criminals" are as pointless as they will be unproductive. Slashing budgets across the board cuts cost effective programs right along with those which are inefficient or ineffective. Candidates and voters must evaluate specific, distinct recommendations for spending cuts and reasonable avenues to enhance government revenues at all levels. The SAGE Commission's recommendations and other ideas in this book are designed to help them to do just that.

In a May, 2008 Executive Order, Governor Jim Gibbons formed the Nevada Spending and Government Efficiency (SAGE) Commission to study the Executive Branch of state government and to make recommendations to him and the Legislature on how to deliver high quality services to citizens for the least amount of money. He appointed 14 senior business leaders from throughout the state to this bipartisan commission: seven Democrats and seven Republicans, ten from the South and four from the North. He asked Republican and Democrat legislative leaders for suggestions on commission makeup, choosing six members from their nominees. This was the strongest, most knowledgeable, most diversified group of business leaders ever brought together as a state commission in Nevada and perhaps in the country. Collectively, they have hundreds of years of experience in managing complex organizations that must be efficient to survive.

At the SAGE Commission's first meeting, the Governor asked members to set aside their individual biases and prejudices and to focus on what was in the best interest of all Nevada citizens. Rather than present a single, voluminous report at the end of its deliberations, he asked the Commission to forward recommendations to him every 90 days so that he could implement needed changes expeditiously in cooperation with the legislature. He did not establish the SAGE Commission to address existing revenue crises. Rather, he sought its help to guide changes needed to ensure the health of state government in the future as the state grows from 3 million to perhaps 5 million over the next decade. He asked commissioners not to concern themselves with the political implications of recommendations, only with their rectitude.

Over 18 months, the SAGE Commission made 44 distinct recommendations that, if fully implemented, will save or enhance state revenues, while resulting in hundreds of new efficiencies in the way Nevada's government delivers services to its citizens. It is noteworthy that all but two of these recommendations were forwarded to the Governor with the unanimous support of the bipartisan Commission.

At some point, a "Grand Bargain" between those who oppose new taxes and those who think Nevada's tax structure is fatally flawed may well be necessary. However, as the following pages will explain, the SAGE Commission has completed some essential first steps by recommending 44 ways to eliminate the use of two billion of those increasingly scarce tax dollars over five years.

The SAGE Commission is justifiably proud of its work, which has not cost the state a single dollar. What is disappointing to them is a reluctance to implement the vast majority of these recommendations. Although the SAGE Commission was not designed to solve the short term revenue crises facing the state, if any of its key recommendations had been enacted in 2009, savings accruing from them would already have been evident in the 2011-13 biennial budget cycle and significant positive impacts could have been expected by 2013-15. This book will analyze the reasons for this inaction and explore some of Nevada's options in the challenging years ahead.

Chapter 2

The Bottom Line:

The 10 Most Important SAGE Recommendations

Public Employee Benefits

By far the most consequential of the recommendations involve the way state employees are paid. As in most government enterprises, over sixty percent of the cost of state government is in compensation to employees. The issue is not salaries. From the testimony and input of nearly thirty organizations and individuals, the SAGE Commission determined that, by and large, state employees are paid a fair salary for the work they perform when gauged against Nevada's private sector. That does not mean that every job is equitable to the private sector or that every job is paid equally. It does mean that, over all, taxpayers pay their state employees a fair salary for the services they receive.

What is not equitable are the benefits provided to state employees, including retirement benefits and contributions to health care for current and retired employees. As reported by Bruce James, "The Commission was shocked to see how the Legislature has allowed these benefits to spin out of control over many years." The result is that taxpayers are now paying about $200 million a year more in benefits to state government employees than if they were employed in the private sector. As the state grows and employees are added, the cost to taxpayers will continue to skyrocket unless the legislature acts now to correct these inequities.

With regard to health care benefits, what the Commission found was that the costs of health insurance are shared between the employee and employer in both the private and public sectors in Nevada. Over a number of years, however, private sector employees have absorbed an increasingly larger share of those costs, and yet Nevada's 26,000 public sector employees covered by its Public Employee Benefits Program (PEBP) have not. Nevada's taxpayers currently pay 95-100% of these "shared" costs for active employees and 85% for their dependents. The current average US cost share percentages in the private sector are 26% for employees and 74% for employers. As noted in the explanation for SAGE Recommendation 12, a Nevada state employee's average monthly contribution for individual health insurance in 2009 is between zero and $28, and between $62 and $194 for dependent coverage for a family of four. A Harrah's employee in 2009 paid between $104 and $323 for approximately the same coverage.

Commissioners recognized that establishing a cost sharing percentage was beyond its competence and that using national data might not reflect Nevada's peculiar economic realities. Recommendation 12, therefore, envisions establishing state health insurance subsidies based on valid comparisons to those paid by Nevada's private sector employers with 100 employees or more, in order to determine a mean average private sector subsidy for all types of health insurance. State subsidies would then be brought to within five percent of this mean. **The estimated savings from this procedure over five years is $322.7 million.**

The Commission found that over 7,800 state retirees were covered under Nevada's PEBP, a figure expected to rise to 8,200 by 2011, and to increase rapidly thereafter, as 43% of current state employees are eligible to retire by 2019. Unlike retirees from the private sector and most states, Nevada public sector retirees receive generous PEBP health care subsidies from the state's general fund. Recommendation 14, therefore, would eliminate all state PEBP subsidies for anyone who retires after July, 2009. These retirees would be eligible to participate in PEBP, but would pay 100% of premiums incurred. **When fully phased in over five years, implementing this recommendation would result in estimated savings to the state of $156.8 million.**

Some commissioners were concerned that possible collusion and manipulation of computations for defined retirement benefits for Nevada's Public Employee Retirement System (PERS) could result in inflated state obligations for 40 years or more. The Commission approved Recommendation 13, which would *prospectively* modify computations for PERS members first employed after July, 2009. These modifications included redefinition of "compensation" for purposes of benefit calculations to base pay only, changing the final average salary definition from the average of the three consecutive highest years to the five consecutive highest years and establishment of a 10% per year compensation cap for these five years.

The recommendation would also eliminate retirement at any age with a prescribed number of years of service by establishing a minimum retirement age of 60. Since PERS is currently underfunded by over $6 billion, the Commission recommended a moratorium on PERS benefit enhancements until the plan is actuarially fully funded for three consecutive years and to sunset any such enhancements in ten years. **If adopted, these changes would result in approximately $100 million in savings over five years.** As partially adopted in SB 427 in the 2009 Legislative Session, beginning in 2010, the five-year savings are estimated at $12 million.

Since some public sector retirees will be paid retirement benefits for over forty years, there is simply no way for the state to continue paying them at existing levels without adversely impacting other important programs. Of course, the real public sector employer is the Nevada taxpayer. As the Economist, sums it up in its July 11, 2009, editorial, today's opaque public sector benefit systems are unfair to taxpayers, who suffer a "triple whammy." First, most of them are enrolled in riskier defined contribution pension schemes where payouts depend on investment performance. Second, employers make smaller contributions to these schemes (and to health care premiums), so benefits are likely to be lower. Third, as well as shouldering more of the burden for their own benefits, private sector workers pay for public sector benefits through their taxes. *There is, in effect, a hidden transfer from private sector workers to their public sector peers...it may amount to as much as 30% of their pay.*

Sunset Committee

The Commission recognized that the Nevada Legislature has met for only a few months each two years for decades and for that reason, the statutes governing the state are a patchwork quilt of overlapping changes, which are seldom subjected to thorough review by those empowered to rationalize and rewrite them. For example, there are currently separate web sites in the state supporting 249 different agencies, commissions, boards or committees. Similarly, tax abatements and earmarks are seldom reviewed to determine whether they continue to meet their intended purpose. Fees established many years ago clearly no longer cover the costs incurred by the state to provide the services for which the fee is assessed. For these reasons, the Commission approved Recommendation 17, which would create and appoint a Sunset Committee to establish a formal review process for, and, on an annual basis, recommend elimination of outdated state entities, abatements, earmarks and exemptions. Although it was impossible to estimate potential savings to Nevada from this recommendation, **the Texas Sunset Commission,** on which this recommendation is based, **has saved that state $737 million in the 21 years it has been operating.**

Inventory of State-Owned Real Estate

Because they have resulted in millions of dollars in near term savings in other states, the Commission approved Recommendation 19, to conduct inventories of all state-owned real estate and buildings, along with a portfolio optimization review of all leased facilities. Private sector real estate entities are willing to perform such inventories without up front fees and legislative approval is not required. Nevada owns surplus real estate acquired for rights-of-way, project expansion or property held as a result of previous transactions. Nevada also leases 1.5 million square feet of space in 212 leases at an annual cost of $28 million. This property is managed by multiple state agencies. The US Office of Management and Budget recommends conducting a detailed review of state-owned real property to distinguish performing from non-performing real estate assets. At least fifteen other states have already performed such inventories and **Virginia has realized savings over ten years of over $70 million.**

Department of Corrections (DOC)

The Commission has made several recommendations regarding Nevada's Department of Corrections. By far the most important in terms of near term savings and ease of implementation is the immediate closure of the Nevada State Prison in Carson City (Recommendation 10). **$19 million in one year and $140 million in five year savings** are estimated by the Commission from closing this prison, which was established in 1862, and remains one of the oldest prisons still operating in the US. Capital improvements required to bring this ancient facility up to existing codes are estimated at a jaw-dropping $40-$50 million.

Three SAGE recommendations were included because of their longer term potential to achieve spending rationalization and enhanced revenues for the state. They are Recommendations 41, establishment of a Nevada State Grants Management Coordinator; 42, which encourages a thorough revision of the state's budget process and 43, which recommends that the state establish overall budget priorities to allocate available funding.

Nevada State Grants Management Coordinator

Nevada is currently ranked 50th by the US Census Bureau for per capita federal aid to states, largely because there is no coordinated grants writing or grants management process in place. Currently, a significant number of opportunities for federal funding are not pursued because of inadequate availability of grants writers and a lack of any communications structure between state agencies and with county, local and non-profit entities. Another census report shows Nevada's return on each federal dollar at 75 cents compared with 95 cents for other western states. Meanwhile, over 85% of Nevada's land is owned and operated by this same federal government. As members of the SAGE Commission and staff were told during an August, 2008, visit to Washington, DC, "Nevada leaves way too much federal money on the table." The **potential return on investment for establishment of a grants coordinator and grants management process is estimated at a 3% increase in federal grant funding in the first year and a 10% increase by year five, or $310 million.**

Budget Reform

Budget reform remains at the core of Nevada's current fiscal problems. The existing process, last revised in 1993, encourages legislative micromanagement and across the board budget cuts, like those taken in 2008 and 2009, which impact essential programs to the same degree as those which are nice to have, or which have outlived their usefulness. No specific approach is favored. Rather, a pilot project at one or more agencies is recommended, since the state clearly needs to make some changes. These projects should present program budgets with clear performance evaluation criteria. Equally important is adoption of overall budget priorities, based on different levels of expected revenues. Working with the governor to establish such priorities is the proper business of legislators. Debating specific budget line items, like copy machines, as is often the case currently, is not.

The existing process of inflating the previous biennium's budget to account for inflation and growth may have sufficed for a state whose revenues were growing each year, but it clearly will no longer work in what may become at best a flat revenue stream for many years to come. More importantly, this budget process has encouraged Nevada's inexperienced, part time legislators to spend every new dollar on new programs at the expense of fully funding significant rainy day accounts. In this way, it is fatally flawed in a state whose tax system is vitally dependent on unreliable and now rapidly falling revenue sources.

Chapter 3

SAGE Research

From the outset, SAGE staff began to review how similar commissions and committees had functioned and what they had found in other states. The Commission was also interested in what had happened to previous efforts to study these issues in Nevada.

One of the first steps was to seek advice from experts in this field, among whom was Paul Posner, a professor at George Mason University in Virginia and an active consultant in the field. Commissioners and staff met with him on its trip to Washington, DC in August, 2008. His overall approach is to divide government fiscal reforms into short, medium and longer terms. He recommended seeking short term savings on the spending side, phasing in medium term management reforms to provide greater flexibility and accountability, while tackling spending and tax compliance issues. In the medium term, he also supported reorganization of state agencies, especially major reductions in boards, commissions and committees. He further recommended performance planning and budgeting, creating a federal aid strategy office and institutionalizing periodic program reviews for major areas on a schedule like the Texas Sunset Commission. Although SAGE did not engage Posner in any formal way, his ideas influenced its recommendations.

Studies in Other States

A review of fiscal policy reform studies reveals that they are typically undertaken at the bottom of a fiscal trough, and usually through hiring an outside consultant for two years at a cost of anywhere from half a million to two million dollars. The consultant produces a two- to three-hundred page document, which is handed over at about the time economic forces have turned around and the state's fiscal crisis is already improving. Whatever recommended reforms might have made sense are never implemented because nobody had time to read the study and political support for reforms had evaporated anyway.

As Dean Martin explained in the old song, *Manana*, "But if we wait a day or two, the rain may go away. And we don't need a window on such a lovely day." The last example of this phenomenon prior to the current steep recession was 2001-2003, in the wake of the 9/11 attacks.

According to a recent analysis by the PEW Center on the States, this process may change radically with this recession. The PEW Center looked closely at ten states, California, Arizona, Nevada, Oregon, Illinois, Michigan, Wisconsin, New Jersey and Rhode Island, based on six factors: high foreclosure rates; increasing joblessness; loss of state revenues; relative size of budget gaps; supermajority requirement for some tax increases or budget bills; and poor money management practices. These states account for more than a third of US population and economic output. They represent a wide variety of fiscal and tax structures, yet their budget gaps were among the worst in the nation, ranging between California at 49% and Oregon at 12%.

States' fiscal situations are expected to worsen when the national economy starts to recover because federal stimulus money will run out and states historically have their worst years shortly after a national recession ends, as they cope with higher Medicaid and other safety net expenses, while revenues continue to lag due to stubborn unemployment.   PEW researchers don't expect recovery from the current fiscal crises in time for these states to avoid significant short, medium and longer-term reforms in their fiscal affairs this time around. They observed four common threads in these states, which could point to vulnerabilities in others, as they try to navigate their way out of the current fiscal crisis:

- **Unbalanced economies.** The economies in these states have depended on a particular industry hit hard in this recession. States cannot change their economies rapidly. They can, however, budget in the future for additional volatility while trying to diversify their economies.

- **Revenues and expenditures out of alignment.** Most states are suffering substantial gaps in this recession, but some have a history of persistent shortfalls, which cannot continue.

- **Limited ability to act.** Lawmakers' latitude to act in these states by raising taxes or cutting spending is limited by law.

- **Putting off tough decisions.** Lawmakers in many of these states "punted their responsibility" by asking voters or governors to make the call or by relying on borrowing or accounting methods and other one-time, short term fixes. Serious fiscal problems cannot be solved without responsible political leadership.

For his part, Mitch Daniels, current Governor of Indiana and former head of the US Office of Management and Budget, says that so many governors are so busy dealing with the current crisis that they haven't checked the long range forecasts. *What we are being hit by isn't a tropical storm that will be followed by sunshine, it's much more likely that we are facing a near permanent reduction in state tax revenues that will require us to reduce the size and scope of our state governments.* It would take national GDP growth of at least twice the historical average to return state tax revenues to their previous long-term trend line by 2012. Those states that raise business taxes will see those businesses go elsewhere. States cannot remain in denial like the federal government by printing money and borrowing from the Chinese. For the states, **"the real world is about to arrive."**

Many state studies were reviewed by SAGE staff. They include North Carolina's 2003 Commission to Promote Government Efficiency and Savings on State Spending; Virginia's 2002 Governor's Commission on Efficiency and Effectiveness; Arizona's 2003 Governor's Efficiency Review Initiative and South Carolina's 2003 Commission on Management, Accountability and Performance. More recent study efforts like Colorado's 2008 Government Efficiency and Management Performance Review (GEM), South Carolina's 2007 Government Efficiency and Accountability Review Committee and Utah's 2008 Working 4 Utah provided SAGE staff some specific ideas regarding issues, study techniques and report formats.

Some conclusions common to many of these studies are that rainy day funds helped during the 2001 recession, along with tax compliance, consolidation of back office functions, outsourcing reforms and real estate management. Techniques which proved successful were: targeting scope to specific areas or operations, iterative reports focusing on specific agencies or issues, creating follow-on entities to implement and track proposals and achieving legislative buy-in and support. As the SAGE process transpired, the importance of each of these techniques became ever more apparent.

Studies in Nevada

Previous Nevada studies on SAGE-related issues date from a 1948 report, entitled "Administrative Reorganization for Effective Government in Nevada," a 1960 "Financing State and Local Government in Nevada" report and similar reports in 1962 and 1992, all of which are gathering dust in the Nevada State Library and Archives.

Studies Commissioned by the Governor

By far the most anticipated recent study was **Governor Kenny Guinn's 2001 Steering Committee to Conduct a Fundamental Review of State Government** .

In January, 2001, this Steering Committee, made up of sixteen people, including five elected officials, three representatives from Nevada counties and school districts, two appointed state officials, a state employee, three private business consultants, a representative of the Nevada Taxpayers Association and a single Reno businessman, submitted

65 recommendations to Governor Kenny Guinn, based on seven meetings over eleven months between September,1999, and October, 2000. Over 200 recommendations were reviewed by the Committee, many of which were initiated by the Executive Branch Internal Audit Division, as well as internal reviews performed by the state agencies themselves.

There were no cost factors attaching either to the implementation or to the follow-on benefits of any of these recommendations, making it difficult to determine which were the most important in terms of their potential savings impact on the cost of Nevada state government. Recurring themes of the study included:

- Retention problems for state employees caused by inadequate training and salaries which fell below those for similar work in local governments;

- Inadequate comprehensive planning for state information technology (IT) functions; and

- Concern among local governments that the state would transfer responsibilities to them without the resources necessary to perform them. Nonetheless, the state's two urban counties, in many cases, were recognized as having far greater resources to provide some services than does the state itself.

Although it is difficult to track the final outcomes on all 65 recommendations, over the intervening period, 2001-2007, it appears that between one half to two thirds of them were not implemented.

Those recommended areas where no definitive action was taken and where the SAGE Commission subsequently determined that significant dollar savings still appeared possible involved:

- The Department of Information Technology.

- Periodic review of Nevada Revised Statutes (state laws) and sunset justification.

- Retention of savings

- Aggressive pursuit of alternative sentencing programs to reduce the fiscal impact of additional capital and operating requirements for state prisons.

In March, 1992, Governor Miller formed a Commission on Governmental Reorganization to promote efficiency, encourage cost savings, enhance accountability and control, improve coordination and reduce redundancy. **The Commission hired KPMG Peat Marwick to conduct this study**, using private sector donations. The Commission's study objectives were to examine the existing structure of the Executive Branch of Nevada state government; identify organizational weaknesses that hamper efficiency, service quality and cost effectiveness and review other states.

A review of the 1992 Executive Branch organization chart revealed 47 agencies reporting to the Governor, including 20 departments, 7 offices and 6 other agencies. There were also 173 state boards and commissions accountable to the governor, with bills before the legislature to create another 23. KPMG adopted several guiding principles for its review, including reducing the governor's span of control; grouping similar functions; shifting the focus of government from inputs to outputs, empowering managers and staff to get the job done and paralleling private sector efforts to streamline management.

Recommendations in KPMG's October, 1992 final report included reducing to 20 the agencies reporting directly to the Governor, including 13 Departments, 3 Boards and 4 Commissions. These reductions were accomplished primarily by grouping existing agencies, boards and commissions into functional areas. Supervisory authority for each was then assigned to entities responsible for those areas.

2008 Executive Branch organizational charts show that some of these 1992 realignment suggestions were implemented. However, even though Governor Miller attempted to reduce the number of boards and commissions, the SAGE Commission found 200 distinct entities listed and discovered 249 separate state government web sites operating largely independently of each other.

Other Relevant Studies Reviewed

The Nevada Taxpayers Association (NTA) 2005 "Overview of Recommendations for a Sound Fiscal Policy" pointed out that since the 1970's, government at all levels has experienced ten to thirteen year cycles when revenues are less than projected, followed by periods of prosperity, when surplus revenues occur. When revenues do not materialize to meet budget expectations, the demand for government services, particularly human services, is greater than normal. Conversely, when greater than anticipated revenues are available, there is pressure on government to increase programs. Meanwhile, at the very time their income is reduced or stagnant, taxpayers are often asked to contribute more to maintain government budgets. Yet, when taxpayers' income is improving, they see no attempt to reduce their tax liability.

Therefore, NTA recommendations encourage strong fiscal responsibility. Throughout, it recommends that higher than expected government revenues be set aside for specific existing categories and not used to start new programs that place enormous demands on future budgets. The same is true of grants and grants management. "While a grant may seem too good to pass up, it may also carry a significant impact on future budget cycles." Existing grants must be continuously reviewed.

Specific NTA recommendations which impacted SAGE research and recommendations were:

- Program or Performance-based budgets should be utilized when possible.

- Outcome based performance indicators should be developed for each program within all departments.

- Both employer and employee should share all retirement contributions.

- Any changes to PERS, such as increased benefits or vesting, should be prohibited until the system is fully funded.

- Change PERS from a defined benefit plan to a defined contribution plan for new employees.

- Eliminate accumulated vacation time and sick leave "buy backs" and provide specific conditions when sick leave or vacation time can be extended beyond the year in which it should be taken.

- Change the procedures by which employee compensation is increased by eliminating longevity pay and changing merit pay to a merit bonus awarded solely on the basis of achievement.

- Cross train employees.

Suffice it to sum up by saying that none of these 2005 NTA recommendations had been implemented by 2009.

In 2008, the Las Vegas Chamber commissioned Hobbs, Ong & Associates and Applied Analysis to analyze state and local fiscal issues including public sector employee compensation levels with particular emphasis on **wage, salary and benefit parity between public and private sector employees in Nevada.**

This analysis, reported in three parts, showed that over 96% of all state and local workers are employed in occupations in which the median pay is higher than that reported for private sector workers in comparable occupations. The average public sector worker in Nevada is paid $47,450 annually and the average private sector worker is paid $37,040, a difference of 28%. It is important to note that SAGE was primarily concerned with state employees, who are paid significantly less than their counterparts working for city and county jurisdictions in Nevada.

For example, state workers were paid at 102% of the national average, ranking 15th nationally among the 50 states and District of Columbia, while "local" public sector employees in Nevada earned 116% of the national averages, making them 8th highest paid in the nation. If Nevada's teachers, who are paid 6.5% less than the national average, are removed from this "local" employee category, the state's local government workers report wages which are 131% of the national average. By comparison, Nevada firefighters reported wages 55% higher than firefighters in all states. Again, the caveat applies that SAGE was not directly involved with either teachers or firefighters.

SAGE was very interested in the state's Public Employees Retirement System (PERS), however. This statewide, defined benefit system required an annual contribution of $1.17 billion in fiscal year 2007, to provide benefits to 35,687 retired workers and set aside funds for 103,693 active employees. Approximately $258 million of this contribution represented payment towards a PERS unfunded accrued liability which is currently $6.3 billion, meaning its retirement system is only 77% fully funded, placing Nevada in the bottom third in the nation in terms of public sector retirement plan funding. *The combination of an aggressive annual retirement benefit factor, no minimum retirement age for retirement with 30 years' service and the relatively low amounts employees are required to contribute toward their own retirement, all applied to higher than average salaries, makes Nevada PERS one of the most generous public employees' retirement systems in the nation.*

The most recent data indicate that Nevada's employer contribution rate of 20.5% for regular employees and 33.5% for fire and police employees rank as the nation's second and third highest among state retirement plans. Approximately 82% of regular employees and 85% of police and fire employees have their PERS contributions paid by their employer in lieu of wage increases. The rationale for this burden sharing was established in the 1970's. The reality of today's higher than average public sector salaries and payment escalations which have often exceeded the rate of inflation have called this practice into serious question in 2009.

This Hobbs & Ong analysis concluded with the observation that transitioning Nevada's PERS from a defined benefit to a defined contribution, even for newly hired employees, *would not be without its challenges. That said, it is difficult to conceive a scenario in which the state would be placed in a worse financial position prospectively as a result of such a transition.*

As the SAGE Commission was in its final deliberations regarding its recommendations on PERS and PEBP (Recommendations 12-15), Commissioner Jan Jones submitted a letter in which she asked for the proposals to be tabled in part because too much Commission emphasis was being placed on this Hobbs and Ong analysis and equal time was not given to other constituencies like the PERS Board, state and local government officials. "It would be unfortunate if our work were dismissed because it appeared that we were not willing to consider perspectives from a wide range of stakeholders." As it happened and as SAGE staff anticipated would be the case on all of its recommendations, the Legislative Counsel Bureau did review and provide broader analysis to the 2009 legislature before it took action on some PERS and PEBP changes which were related to SAGE Recommendations 12-15. In addition, Commissioner Jones was gracious in helping SAGE staff acquire actual data from a Nevada private sector corporation, Harrah's, regarding its employee-employer contribution rates for health insurance.

It is important to note that SAGE Recommendation 12 does not prescribe employer subsidy limits. Rather, it says these subsidies should be brought into "approximate parity with those provided to their employees by Nevada's private sector employers."

Although the Commission had determined that Executive Branch reorganization was likely to exceed its resources and timelines, it invited **UNR Professor Eric Herzik to provide a non-prescriptive, theoretical, academic analysis of Nevada's government organization at its May, 2009 Commission meeting.** Dr Herzik made a number of important points, including that:

- Organizational inefficiency is usually the purview of the legislature.

- To fundamentally change how government grows, delivers services and conducts business you must change how government operates, not just where it operates and to whom it reports. If you want governments to change, you must change the incentives of its employees.

- Public and private management are alike in all unimportant aspects, according to Wallace Sayre.

- Both private and public sector structures respond to need, but the private sector metric is profit. The public sector defines "need" as constituents served.

- The "value environment" in the public sector includes equity over efficiency, neutrality in hiring and service delivery, accountability to multiple overseers and representativeness. No one of these values trumps any of the others.

He noted that key differences which usually make government services less efficient include fragmentation of authority to make decisions and enforce them, greater public scrutiny, lack of market pressure, personnel constraints, performance measurement, and services which are mandated by a legislature, court or the public. Hence, the public wants more and expects more because it has no idea of the costs involved. Elected officials want to be responsive, not efficient. Once services (or commissions) are in place, they have constituents. There are few constituents for change other than expansion. Therefore, the problem isn't efficiency, but that the incentives pursue all the values except efficiency.

So what might be done? According to Osborne and Gaebler, authors of Reinventing Government:

- Change the incentives. The current incentives are all in the direction of not making mistakes. For public managers, following the rules means you are safe. Allow failure of some initiatives and eliminate creating a statute for every mistake or circumstance.

- Power down. Decentralize authority.

- Develop a system of retained savings for frugal managers.

- Be careful that performance indicators measure what counts, not things you can count.

- Promote competitive government which allows government either to buy private sector options or compete in private sector activities.

- Charge fair prices for all government services.

- Limit the rules and give managers the flexibility to manage their own budgets.

In most of these areas, the experts agree with state employees (see Chapter 7). However, elected officials are responsive to the public focus on cost controls that dictate what bureaucrats can spend on every item, so they cannot possibly waste, misuse or steal taxpayer's money. This focus on "protecting the taxpayer from government" results in government spending $1.25 for every $1 in value the taxpayer receives.

As summarized by the PEW Center on the States, 2009, Nevada's population mushroomed 30 percent between 2000 and 2008, compared with 8 percent growth for the rest of the country. However, most of that growth was driven by people under six and over 65, leaving the state to finance public services like K-12 education and long term health care with shrinking gaming and sales taxes. Meanwhile, social costs are adding up. Homeless children in Las Vegas rose by 42% and Nevada leads the nation in the number of uninsured children. Food bank demand went up 68% and state officials are predicting 43,000 more Nevada residents will be on Medicaid. Meanwhile, only Hawaii depends more on tourist dollars than Nevada where $6 of every $10 in state tax revenue comes from gaming or sales, and year on year revenue has fallen for a record two consecutive years. However, changing Nevada's tax structure is a constitutional process, which would take a minimum of five years and approval by voters in two successive general elections.

Finally, throughout its research efforts SAGE staff was cognizant of repeated advice that efficiency gains alone, or even when coupled with tax increases, were unlikely to plug major budget holes. **State governments might have to shed some functions altogether.**

Chapter 4

Methodology and Recommendations

The SAGE Commission took responsibility for reviewing all state government entities in the Executive Branch which fall under the control of the governor. Excluded were the Nevada System of Higher Education, K-12 education, constitutional officers, legislative and judicial entities. Even with these restrictions, the tasks confronting volunteer SAGE Commissioners and their three-person paid staff were so complex that completing them within the time frame and with the resources available required judicious application of workable methodologies and organization. It was decided to approach the challenge in three ways simultaneously.

Horizontal Recommendations

The first was to examine each entity of state government within the SAGE mandate *horizontally*, across the "silos" of individual state government departments to allow each of them an opportunity to participate in helping to make state government more efficient by identifying and implementing best practices in broad functional areas of state expenditures such as: personnel, information technology, purchasing and procurement, real estate, operations and maintenance, energy, printing, health insurance, and workforce education and training. The Commission began its work by inviting agency directors to submit their ideas in each area. It then impaneled working "task forces," made up of a commissioner, a SAGE staff member, a "senior advisor," borrowed from the private sector, and other experts, both from government and from the private sector, to review the ideas and to develop a best practices plan for each.

Horizontal task forces were eventually created and active in personnel, information technology, purchasing/procurement, real estate and budget processes. Meeting simultaneously, as task forces completed deliberations, staff drafted proposals on individual issues, which were then brought before the full Commission. They were reviewed, revised and either rejected or approved by a vote of the Commission, then submitted to the Governor for his review and possible implementation, working with the legislature where required by relevant law.

Note: The following summaries of SAGE Commission recommendations indicate a number which corresponds to the final recommendation, as approved by the SAGE Commission. All 44 recommendations in their entirety can be seen at the Appendix. Where available, estimated five-year savings of each recommendation are shown in bold face.

Personnel

11. Evaluate a four-day work week for all non-essential Nevada State employees beginning October, 2009. **$50 million**

12. Establish state health insurance subsidies based on valid comparisons to those paid by Nevada's private sector employers to determine a mean average private sector subsidy. State subsidies would then be brought to within five percent of this mean. **$322.7 million**

13. Modify retirement benefit computations for Public Employee Retirement System (PERS) members first employed after July, 2009, to redefine "compensation" to base pay only, changing the final average salary definition from the three consecutive highest years to the five consecutive highest years, establish a 10% per year compensation cap for these five years and establish a minimum retirement age of 60. **$100 million**

14. Eliminate all state PEBP subsidies for anyone who retires after July, 2009. These retirees would be eligible to participate in PEBP, but would pay 100% of premiums incurred. **$156.8 million**

15. Modify retirement benefits for all PERS members effective July 1, 2009, if legally permissible.

38. Require directors of cabinet level departments to establish and implement cross training programs for their employees where feasible and practical.

Information Technology

25. Nevada's Department of Information Technology (DoIT) should implement and maintain an Enterprise Web Content Management System capable of hosting agency Web content and Web based applications, providing a single point of access for Nevada's citizens. **$1.5 million**

26. Establish a common email platform for all Executive Branch Agencies. **$750,000**

32. Nevada's information technology future should be defined through a comprehensive strategic planning process organized and developed by the State Information Technology Advisory Board (ITAB).

34. Revise statute language so that State agencies, boards, and commissions in the Executive Department are not exempt from using DoIT professional services except for those infrastructures, enterprise architectures, facilities and personnel required for control of the specialized mission of the enterprise.

35. Solicit recommendations for a common telecommunications platform for all Executive branch state agencies and invite the Judicial and Legislative branches, Constitutional Officers, the Nevada System of Higher Education (NSHE) and cities and counties throughout the State to participate.

Vertical Recommendations

Secondly, SAGE Commission staff identified those agencies included in the Commission's scope of work responsible for 80% of state government spending. These agencies were then examined vertically, within their own spending silos, for possible reductions and efficiencies. Due to its size and complexity, three task forces were created for the Department of Health and Human Services (HHS): HHS Regulatory & Standardization Issues, HHS Mental Health Services and HHS Health Care Systems. Other vertical review task forces were created for Corrections/Parole and Probation (DOC/PP), Transportation (NDOT) and Motor Vehicles (DMV). The task force process was essentially identical for both horizontal and vertical reviews of state government.

Health and Human Services (30% of state spending)

1. Centralize billing for third party pay services in Mental Health and Developmental Services (MHDS). **$12 million** (implemented)

2. Staffing ratios in state operated psychiatric facilities need to be evaluated against private sector and national norms. **$36 million** (implemented)

3. Implement Managed Care for the Aged, Blind and Disabled (ABD) groups in the Medicaid program in Clark and Washoe Counties, and expand Managed Care to women and children in four rural counties. **$36.5 million**

4. Acquire Distributive School Funding (DSA) for the Nevada Youth Training Center (NYTC) at Elko, which is currently a high-school-like facility that is paid for with state general funds. **$2.3 million**

6. Identify and coordinate the activities of all departments, agencies and institutions of the Executive Department that administer programs for the treatment of drug and alcohol abuse, or which provide funding to local governments for such programs.

8. Examine ways to use the Indigent Accident Fund/Supplemental Relief Fund for federal matching funds to the Medicaid and Nevada Check Up programs. **$250 million**

44. Increase efforts to reduce costs for prescription drugs in the departments of Health and Human Services and Corrections by continuing ongoing programs and investigating new initiatives. **$27.8 million**

Corrections (4% of state spending)

10. Close the Nevada State Prison in Carson City immediately. **$140 million**

31. Authorize the Department of Corrections (DOC) to establish an intermediate sanction facility for certain probation violators and offenders, who are determined to be substance abusers. **$280 million**

36. Explore the possibility of an exchange of Ely State Prison and Lovelock Corrections Center to private corrections companies in return for construction of similar facilities located within existing large population centers.

37. The Department of Corrections should issue a request for proposals to evaluate the costs and benefits of privatization of inmate medical and mental health care and the provision of pharmaceutical services. **$24.1 million**

Nevada Department of Transportation (NDOT 9% of state spending)

20. A distance-based user fee pilot program should be designed, supported and funded for NDOT and the Regional Transportation Commission (RTC) of Washoe County.

29. Nevada Revised Statutes regarding design-build contracts should be expanded to allow both an increased number of such projects per year and a significantly lower dollar threshold limit on such contracts.

39. The Nevada Department of Transportation should perform a detailed analysis and review of all existing NDOT maintenance stations throughout the state with a view to eliminating or consolidating some stations. $4.4 million

40. NDOT should commission a study to develop decision factors for outsourcing roadway maintenance rather than providing it using NDOT crews.

Diagonal (Organizational) Recommendations

Third, the commission staff originally sought to undertake a thorough examination of the structure and makeup of all the entities of the executive branch of state government, with a particular emphasis on discovering redundancies, duplication and obsolescence among and between them. As noted elsewhere, there are at least 200 separate entities shown on current Nevada state government organization charts and 249 separate web sites. Therefore, there are clear prospects for significant spending cuts and efficiencies.

However, this *"diagonal"* review was soon recognized as simply too ambitious for staff and commission to undertake under its constraints of time and resources. Moreover, many previous recommendations to reorganize state government and reduce the numbers of boards, commissions, councils and committees had met with little or no support from the legislature or its constituents. The commission believes that its previously described recommendation to create a "Sunset Committee" will rationalize and reduce this proliferation of state organizations over time.

5. Complete the downsizing of the DMV night shift while maintaining the goal of a five-day title turnaround time. **$470,000** (implemented)

17. Create and appoint a Sunset Committee to establish a formal review process for, and recommend elimination on an annual basis of, outdated state entities, abatements, earmarks and exemptions.

28. Request appointment of an Interim Legislative Committee to study the Public Works process.

33. Change the Interim Finance Committee (IFC) oversight thresholds to amounts more relative to the dollar amounts of current budget totals as well as government and non-government grants.

Revenue Enhancements

Cognizant of potentials where Nevada was "leaving too much federal money on the table," which were brought to the attention of the commission and staff during its fact finding trip to Washington, DC, in August, 2008, staff began to add a category of examination to the work of its task forces involving potential enhancements to the revenues available to the state that did not involve new taxes. These "revenue enhancements" became an important category of SAGE recommendations, in addition to those discovered during its extensive "horizontal" and "vertical" examinations.

7. Establish steeply discounted digital printing, copying, finishing, delivery and other services by vendors on-line and at any of their outlets throughout the State, using access cards which document and bill all transactions electronically. **$3.5 million**

9. Review available options and recommend the most cost effective solution for the DMV auto insurance verification program to reduce the number of uninsured motorists currently driving illegally in Nevada to 10%, or less. **$20.9 million** (implemented)

16. The Senior Citizens Property Tax Assistance Program should be administered and fully funded by the various counties, which actually collect property taxes. **$30 million**

18. All state agencies should review the fees charged for services to ensure the fees cover the costs of providing the services. Fees and costs should be reviewed every two years. **$5 million**

19. Conduct inventories of all state-owned real estate and buildings, along with a portfolio optimization review of all leased facilities.

21. Provide State financial support to create a Nevada-oriented marketing and outreach program to supplement the national census advertising campaign. **$79.6 million** (implemented by Governor and legislature)

22. Reinstate the requirement that Proof of Insurance from a licensed Nevada insurance company be presented to the Nevada Department of Motor Vehicles (DMV) for new vehicle registrations and establish a DMV website to facilitate issuance of all temporary Proof of Insurance cards. **$21.5 million** (approved by legislature and Governor)

23. License applicants who return for additional drive tests beyond a second try should be charged a duplicate retest fee. **$3.7 million** (partially implemented)

24. The State should make statutory changes to the interest rates paid on overpayment of taxes and charged on underpayment of taxes for both individuals and businesses by adopting the Internal Revenue Service index and adjusting it periodically.

27. Nevada should significantly improve its state level energy conservation efforts by enforcing its existing energy conservation plan and revising that plan consistent with 2009 organizational, financial, statutory and technical realities.

30. Define "fees" as charges made to recover the cost of operating the program or providing the service, including indirect cost (overhead), and "costs" as the direct cost of the program or service plus its allocable portion of indirect cost.

41. Create a Nevada State Grants Management Coordinator to enhance opportunities for federal funding by monitoring grants writing and grants management, insuring availability of grants writers and establishing a communications structure between state agencies and with county, local and non-profit entities. **$310 Million**

42. Undertake pilot projects at one or more state agencies to implement changes in Nevada's budget system. These projects should present program budgets with clear performance evaluation criteria and help to establish funding priorities based on different levels of expected revenues.

43. A method of establishing budget priorities based on different levels of expected revenues should be adopted.

Chapter 5

Reports, Finance and Governance

Reports

In the hope that SAGE reports would be read, staff kept recommendations to one page and submitted them every 90 days, something that had not been tried in any other similar study. We realized that very little research or background information could be included, but we knew that most recommendations would have to be approved by the legislature and would, therefore, be thoroughly researched by the Legislative Counsel Bureau, regardless of the level of SAGE staff effort.

Finance and Governance

The Nevada SAGE Commission Inc. was organized as a Nevada non-profit corporation and received 501(c)3 charitable status from the Internal Revenue Service. This Commission was funded entirely from the private sector. No state funds have been spent to cover its estimated expenses of over $350,000.

Contributions, when received, were handled under a fund agreement with the Community Foundation of Western Nevada.

Chapter 6

The Environment

The activities of the SAGE Commission took place during the deepest US recession since the Great Depression and the worst economic environment on record in Nevada. Every aspect of its activities was affected.

Fundraising was virtually non-existent. From day one, staff was very frugal with each dollar loaned to SAGE by its Chairman, Bruce James. We created virtual offices from our own homes and charged nothing to Commission accounts except necessities such as air travel to bi-monthly Commission meetings in Las Vegas. We borrowed meeting facilities from the University of Nevada, Reno and from the State when in Las Vegas. Staff took significant pay cuts beginning in August, 2009. Meanwhile, although committed to SAGE work, Commissioners were constantly consumed with various impacts of the recession on their normal daily workloads.

Despite Governor Gibbons' admonition to the Commission to simply get it right and let him handle the politics, the political environment of the 2009 legislative session was so poisoned by partisan rhetoric from both sides that the few SAGE recommendations, which actually made it to any sort of hearing, were dead on arrival. Some legislative leaders apparently viewed the entire SAGE enterprise as a stalking horse for the Governor's "no new taxes pledge" and treated anyone associated with SAGE accordingly.

Initial working relationships between SAGE and Governor's staff, which were becoming closer, had, by the middle of 2009, evaporated. By then, every policy position in the Governor's immediate office had changed incumbents at least once. Although Jim Gibbons remained both passionate and articulate regarding the importance of SAGE and its work, he knew that he could implement very few of its recommendations alone and was either unable or unwilling to negotiate with the legislature to do so. In fairness to everyone involved, however, most SAGE recommendations were not finalized in time to receive thorough legislative review and action in 2009.

Public Relations

The stage for SAGE public relations was set on its first day. After the May 7, 2008, Executive Order signing, failed gubernatorial candidate, Dina Titus, commented to a reporter that since (Governor Gibbons) had handpicked commissioners with his agenda, "I don't think it will be credible." In fact, Gibbons appointed eight members and asked legislative leaders like Titus for recommendations for another six. In Jon Ralston's May, 2008, Las Vegas Sun column supporting formation of the SAGE Commission, he said, "I had no idea my word processor would allow me to type kudos and Gibbons in the same sentence." In so doing, he and Titus had set in stone two SAGE public relations problems. First, SAGE was viewed by many simply as part of Governor Gibbons' "no new taxes" strategy. Second, getting the facts straight in the few SAGE news stories which made it into print would be a continuing challenge.

There were early and inaccurately reported leaks to Ralston and others, which confused SAGE staff "Proposals" and Commission-approved "Recommendations." Some reporters, like Brendan Riley of the Associated Press, were more diligent than others in seeking clarifications. Most early headlines called SAGE an "Anti-waste panel," an aphorism which stuck, even though it was a largely inaccurate description of the SAGE Commission's work.

SAGE resources simply could not support hiring even a part time public relations professional. However, throughout its existence, SAGE maintained a web site, www.sagenevada.org, where all relevant information was readily available, including recommendations, meeting dates and agendas, press releases, commissioner biographies and contact information. SAGE's multi-talented General Manager, Suzanne Kilgore, issued professional-quality press releases for each of the Commission's six quarterly reports to the Governor.

Chairman Bruce James spoke at a variety of events throughout the state. He gave interviews when asked, including a thirty minute, August, 2008, taped session with Tad Dunbar, which subsequently appeared on Reno's NBC affiliate TV show, *The Dunbar Report*. Unfortunately, Bruce's appearances, a good source of "earned media," were seldom covered by anyone in the media. Other commissioners and staff members were occasionally subjects of short news items and provided background material for the few articles and commentaries which were produced about SAGE.

SAGE had its proponents, to be sure. Political activist Chuck Muth was an early and outspoken supporter of SAGE's work, arguing that government efficiency was an oxymoron. The way to fix it was to reduce its size. Both the Las Vegas and Reno Chambers of Commerce were supportive and received media coverage of that support. Daryl Drake, a contributor and SAGE friend wrote columns and provided backgrounders to those who would listen to him. In May, 2009, Chairman James published a seminal column in the *Las Vegas Review Journal* outlining accurately the SAGE position on public employee benefits after months of public posturing by those public employee organizations which sought to misrepresent this position.

Perfunctory Google and Yahoo searches show over one hundred media entries regarding the SAGE Commission and its activities during the eighteen months of its existence. Finally, despite its public relations impediments, by the end of the 2009 legislative session, with its mostly disappointing results for SAGE recommendations, Jane Ann Morrison, a *Review Journal*, columnist wrote about the SAGE Commission's "successes" to that point. "Even if lawmakers didn't go as far as SAGE commissioners wanted, commissioners have made progress in saving you money and they are only half finished," she wrote. And, she admitted, "I started as a skeptic."

2008 General Elections and 2009 Legislative Session

By far the biggest distraction to the SAGE Commission's work during its eighteen month life was the over one-third of that life which took place during the elections of 2008 and the 2009 Nevada legislative session which followed. Elections have consequences. Riding President

Barak Obama's coattails and capitalizing on local issues, the Nevada Assembly ended up with a veto-proof majority of 28 Democrats and 14 Republicans. Although not veto proof, a long-standing Republican majority in the Senate was reversed with the election of twelve Democrats and nine Republicans. Barbara Buckley was elected Speaker of the Assembly and Steven Horsford replaced perennial Republican Senate Majority Leader Bill Raggio in that position. Raggio had a well-earned reputation as a moderate dealmaker between the two political parties. His loss was quickly evident as the Democrats decided to go to war with the Republican Governor who was all too happy to oblige.

However, consequences also have consequences. Having rejected the Governor's "draconian" budget out of hand, Democrat leadership found that it had to create a balanced budget of its own. Although numerous hearings revealed damaging impacts on recipients of proposed reductions, the almost $3 billion deficit remained. None of the Democrat majority had called for any new taxes during their campaigns. Few liberal legislators supported even trimming the growth of government that had occurred throughout the boom years, let alone the size and scope of its functions. Some talked of a finding a "balanced" state tax structure that wasn't affected by the global fiscal crisis, but 49 of the 50 states were already suffering fiscal problems equal to or worse than Nevada's and many were already making huge budget cuts. Nevada has always exported its taxes to its visitors. The largest tax increase approved in this legislative session and the third largest in Nevada history was an increase in room taxes designed not to "restructure" Nevada's taxes, but to load more of its tax burden onto these same tourists.

In the end, the 2009-2011 $6.9 billion budget was balanced through $1 billion in across-the-board spending cuts, $1 billion in new taxes and $1 billion in federal economic stimulus dollars. Governor Gibbons vetoed 41 bills, including this state budget, the most since 1864, Nevada's first year as a state. The impasse between them continued to the end with the legislature setting its own record for veto overrides. However, two more years of declines in gaming revenues and double-digit drops in sales and use tax collections have opened a $3 billion hole in the budget the Governor and lawmakers will confront again in January, 2011.

Meanwhile, the initial position of the SAGE Commission and its staff was that its work was designed to deal with spending and efficiency savings with a 5-10 year time horizon, not to try to fix the near term crisis facing Nevada. However, during its August, 2008, visit to Washington, DC, SAGE commissioners and staff agreed with Commissioner Steve Hill that the Commission risked becoming "irrelevant" if it were not prepared to bring some of its recommendations forward in time for the 2009 legislative session.

Consequently, staff turned immediately to proposals it had initially put on the back burner. New proposals, particularly in the PEBP and PERS areas took high priority. An inordinate amount of staff time was expended to bring these proposals before the Commission so that they could be included in the December, 2008, 90-day report to the Governor. He was then able to include any SAGE recommendations which he approved in his budget submission to the legislature.

The result of these four months of special effort on the part of staff and commissioners was eight new recommendations, which were estimated to yield nearly $700 million in savings to the state over five years. Many were contentious and two became the only SAGE recommendations which were not unanimously approved by the bipartisan Commission. Regarding the political process, SAGE moved from being irrelevant to being ignored. Some legislators appeared to treat these SAGE recommendations simply as attempts by the Governor to interfere in their functions. Legislators listened politely to testimony on the few SAGE recommendations which came before them in legislative committee hearings before disregarding them.

Fifteen states prohibit legislators from being employed by their state governments, according to the National Conference on State Legislatures. Nine forbid them from holding any other state or local government job. Seven states allow such employment as long as the lawmaker isn't paid for both his government job and legislative position. Six states prevent legislators from holding any government jobs that could conflict with their duties as legislators.

Nevada is among twenty states which have no such restrictions. It also has no restrictions on legislators who are retired from state or local government positions or whose spouses currently hold or are retired from such positions.

Conflicts of interest in the legislature should be resolved in favor of Nevada's taxpaying citizens. Those who benefit directly or indirectly from the State's retirement and health care systems should not be allowed to vote on them. As a minimum they should recuse themselves from doing so. The total number of Nevada's 63 legislators who are conflicted in some way is subject to interpretation. What is not is that none of them recused themselves from voting on SAGE recommendations regarding Nevada state employee benefits.

So, by the end of the 2009 session, SAGE's worst nightmare, the outcome that all of its procedures were designed to prevent, had come to pass. SAGE had become irrelevant to Nevada and its fiscal crises. The question that remains is simple. Can SAGE and its recommendations for $2 billion in savings or enhanced revenues for state government be resurrected? Without achieving legislative support in the 2011 Legislative Session the answer is clearly, "no." However, according to Nevada's experts, fiscal crises in 2011 will be as bad or worse as in 2009. Perhaps other legislators and governors can find ways to craft a "Grand Bargain" between spending restraint and new revenues using completed SAGE recommendations to help them.

Chapter 7

Interaction With State Employees

From day one, Chairman James and I knew that without the support of state employees, we could not successfully conduct or complete the Commission's work. Especially with such a small SAGE staff, the full cooperation of state employees at every level, from the governor's office to corrections officers was imperative. Attitudes, perceived and actual, were crucial to achieving such cooperation. We quickly came to see the process at close range. Nevada's legislature has tended to treat state employees as though they can not be trusted by micromanaging their work through budget processes designed to protect taxpayers from employee decisions.

SAGE commissioners and staff took a different view from the outset. We believed Nevada had good employees working in faulty systems. We felt that berating them about waste would suggest that we thought they were either incompetent, dishonest or both. After the Commission's first meeting, Chairman Bruce James sent a letter to the 17 Department Directors who comprise the Governor's cabinet. In it he said, in part:

> *"The answers to how we can improve operations and reduce costs will most likely come from you and your staff. By looking across all operations we should be helpful to you by identifying best practices that can be employed throughout the executive branch and we may be able to offer specific guidance for your operations. We do this in the spirit of cooperation and consideration of the unique requirements you may have. But, we intend the end result to be better services to citizens at less cost, which you need to communicate and reinforce with your employees. The Commission wants to help you implement your best ideas.*

"The best ideas are not going to come from 14 wise-people (commissioners) sitting around a table. They're going to come from you and the thousands of dedicated state employees. Our job is to help you achieve success in streamlining your operations by taking unnecessary costs out of running government and by achieving ever greater customer satisfaction."

Shortly afterwards, as Executive Director, I followed up with a second letter to each Director designed to encourage responses and provide some clarification, since SAGE was so new. My letter said that:

As one on the front lines of our State government's operations, directors are in the best position to know what can or should be changed to make state government more efficient in effort spent and services delivered to their fellow Nevadans. We are aware of the cuts directors have endured to their programs simply to balance budgets for this fiscal year. We know that they are struggling to complete their budget requests, while wrestling with other duties. However, we also think that this is an opportune time to accomplish some changes that may not otherwise be possible for years, if ever.

We are not seeking more budget cuts. Rather, we are asking for suggestions on procedures, processes or services that directors and staff would like to see changed. We want to know how each department could perform its services for less money by making such changes, but doing so is not within its authority. Directors probably find little time to spend on creatively thinking through the way their departments operate. Now, we are asking them to do just that. SAGE is not about spending even less money on necessary programs. SAGE is about re-thinking programs, how Nevada provides essential services, implementing new productivity tools, or other new ideas.

You and your Division administrators can help the SAGE Commission with the questions it must address:

- *Is this a service or function that government should be providing on behalf of its citizens?*

- *Should it be provided by State government?*

- *Should State government provide the service itself or buy it?*

- *Should providing that service by State government be accomplished in some ways differently than it is being provided now?*

The lack of responses to these two letters was somewhat discouraging. However, we already knew there would be resistance to establishing an early and close partnership with an organization which seemed to be saying, "We are going to report directly to the Governor and we are here to help you." We did more than write letters. By November, 2008, the Deputy Director and I had made over thirty separate visits to a variety of department directors and other employees, following up on our search for ideas.

On July 8, 2009, we began a task we also knew from the outset that we simply must undertake, when I met with the University of Nevada's Center for Design Research and Analysis (CDRA) to begin the process of designing, conducting and evaluating a comprehensive survey of all state employees. By September, we had commissioned UNR's CDRA to conduct the survey. From an initial contact list, UNR surveyors reached 10,324 state employees. Of those, 3,762 completed the survey and 2,558 answered this open-ended question:

"Please provide any ideas you may have to save money, bring in more revenue, provide better customer service, and to make state government more effective or efficient with respect to your immediate general work environment. Please be as specific as possible, as these comments are extremely valuable to us."

UNR and SAGE staffs were impressed with the volume and overall thoughtfulness of the responses in general and many of them in particular. Most respondents agreed that there were many prospects for providing state government services more cost effectively.

Employees were acutely aware that personnel costs are central to the costs of state government. A major portion of employee respondent suggestions addressed personnel costs in some fashion. For example:

- forfeiting some portion of employee pay to meet crises (e.g., longevity pay).

- unpaid days off.

- hiring "less than full time" employees.

- time clocks to document actual time worked.

- eliminating overtime and sick pay abuses and establishing accountability for both.

- making classification changes to eliminate eligibility for overtime pay.

- reducing the numbers of middle managers and "deputies."

- reviewing the classified-unclassified employee threshold.

- creating a "merit raise" system with COLA increases.

- increasing the numbers of "at will" employees.

- making it easier to terminate unproductive employees.

In that same context, there was overwhelming approval of the 4-day work week concept. Many respondents added ideas such as:

- flex schedules and job sharing

- telecommuting and working from home.

Respondents were savvy on broader budget issues, as well. They provided many examples of the wastefulness involved in preventing department use of savings they generated for other useful purposes and recommended:

- program versus line item budgeting.

- allowing department heads reprogramming authority for saved funding.

- performance based budgeting.

In related comments, respondents made uniformly negative comments regarding the entire Interim Finance Committee (IFC) process. They argued it was overly bureaucratic, that it wasted senior leadership time by requiring their attendance for long, unproductive periods during IFC meetings and that the IFC process precluded efficient handling of federal grants. They recommended:

- annual legislative sessions.

- changing thresholds and criteria to preclude IFC review of routine expenditures.

Employees felt the state was doing far too little to implement any real energy conservation system. They recommended:

- surveys by utilities providers to seek ways to save energy and dollars.

- installing automatic systems which will shut down electronic devices when they are not being used on evenings and weekends.

- following existing state policies regarding seasonal thermostat settings.

Respondents felt there was significant duplication of work and that some consolidation and reorganization of agencies and other entities made sense.

There was a wide variety of recommendations to save money and employee time in travel related activities. Among these were:

- state vehicle use by employees for travel to and from work needed to be reviewed and monitored more closely for possible abuse.

- out of state travel should be closely scrutinized.

- air fares, particularly multiple trips by multiple employees required careful evaluation. Could the state contract for air service more cost effectively?

- evaluate leasing versus purchase of state vehicles.

- video conferencing and teleconferencing versus personnel travel.

Furthermore, employees from a variety of departments favored centralization of IT operations statewide.

Respondents wanted all fees charged by the state to reflect what the services provided actually cost the state.

Respondents would rather explore Yucca Mountain as a revenue source than lose their jobs.

This last comment summarizes an overall understanding by most employees that in the face of severe fiscal constraints, many of their jobs were at risk. They were providing reasons not to adopt the usual across the board approach to such cuts, arguing effectively that more reasoned, distinct steps were available.

Many of the trends discovered in staff analysis of these open-ended survey responses fit nicely into the ongoing work of SAGE Task Forces and many of these found their way into the final 44 Commission-approved Recommendations to the Governor.

Chapter 8

Meetings

The initial meeting of the SAGE Commission took place in the Media Room of the Capitol Annex in Carson City on June 26, 2008. Governor Gibbons addressed the Commission before the meeting was called to order. He thanked commissioners for their willingness to volunteer and explained how important its work would be in the light of the difficult fiscal situation already confronting Nevada.

After self-introductions by commissioners, a briefing by Patty Cafferata, Executive Director Nevada Commission on Ethics, explained the differences between ethics in business and ethics in government. She was followed by George Taylor, Senior Deputy Attorney General, who distributed and reviewed information regarding Nevada's Open Meeting Law. The first statute of the Open Meeting Law is that all deliberations and action should be taken in public.

As a private non-profit entity, the SAGE Commission is technically not a part of Nevada's government and Cafferata and Taylor agreed that it was not, therefore, subject to Nevada's Ethics or Open Meeting statutes. However, Chairman James made it clear at this initial meeting that commissioners would be expected to disclose any conflicts of interest and staff would follow all the provisions of Open Meeting law statutes.

Deputy Director and former State Budget Director, Perry Comeaux then reviewed the state budget, followed by Commissioner and former Assemblyman David Goldwater, who provided a briefing on the state budget process. Staff views on SAGE study methodologies were then reviewed with commissioners, initial task forces established and a tentative meeting schedule adopted. It was decided to alternate meetings between Reno and Las Vegas every other month. Las Vegas meetings were held in available rooms in the Grant Sawyer building, while those in Reno used available facilities provided by UNR.

The July 24, meeting in Las Vegas was given over to a thorough review of the Department of Health and Human Services, which, at $5 billion in operations and general funding, is by far the largest Executive Branch Department. Michael Willden, HHS Director, provided an overview before introducing Administrators Charles Duarte, Health Care Financing and Policy, Harold Cook, Mental Health and Developmental Services and Diane Comeaux, Child and Family Services.

By September 2008, agendas generally involved discussion and assignment of particular issues to specific task forces; review and update of task force activities by task force chairpersons or staff members; and discussion, amendment and approval of staff or task force proposals to be included in the quarterly SAGE report to the Governor. The October 24, 2008 meeting was largely devoted to draft proposals on the Public Employee Benefits Program (PEBP) and Public Employee Retirement System (PERS). Leslie Johnstone, PEBP Executive Officer and Randy Kerner, PEBP Board Chairman briefed the Commission, followed by Dana Bilyeu, PERS Executive Officer and Ken Lambert, PERS Investment Officer. There were nearly one hundred observers at this meeting and several of them spoke regarding the effects SAGE proposals could have on state employee benefits.

At the December 4, 2008, meeting, Russell McAllister, representing professional firefighters and Ron Dreher, representing professional police associations, both pointed out the importance of keeping these two professions youthful and vigorous through early PERS retirement opportunities.

On January 22, 2009, Jodi Stephens, Legislative Director for the Governor reviewed with the Commission the twelve of nineteen SAGE recommendations which had been included in the Governor's Budget which was sent to the legislature.

At the March 26, meeting, Cathy Illian, US Census Bureau Regional Director, explained how the census each ten years determines federal funding allocations to the states for the following ten years. David Byerman, US Commerce Department Chief Government Liaison for Nevada, pointed out that the census could garner Nevada another electoral seat if state funds were invested to insure a more accurate count at the local level. Conversely, an undercount could cost Nevada $16 million per year for ten years.

At the April 23, 2009, meeting, Marty Bibb, Executive Director, Retired Public Employees of Nevada elicited a clarification from commissioners and staff that the SAGE PEBP recommendation included a provision designed to protect low- income retired public employees. On June 25, Assembly Speaker Barbara Buckley supported the Commission's interaction with legislative leaders to increase legislators' understanding of the rationale behind its recommendations.

At its July 23, meeting, Attorney Craig Engle and former Washington, DC Mayor Anthony Williams spoke to the Commission regarding federal funding opportunities in addition to the American Recovery and Reinvestment Act (stimulus funding).

On September 24, Ray Bacon, Nevada Association of Manufacturers, encouraged defining the relationship between local, state and federal governments, suggesting the SAGE Commission recommend an Interim Legislative Study to consider these relationships and amendments to the budget process.

The SAGE Commission's final meeting was in December, 2009 and its Final Report was presented to Governor Gibbons by Chairman Bruce James on January 7, 2010.

Chapter 9

SAGE People

SAGE Commissioners

Commission Chairman Bruce R. James, President of Nevada New-Tech, Inc., **former U.S. Public Printer, a Presidential appointment**. Bruce was not only the inspiration and financier for the SAGE Commission, he did an excellent job of chairing its five-hour meetings. As chair, he constantly sought to achieve consensus among this bipartisan Commission. He elicited comments, explored compromise language and kept discussions on point. He helped commissioners steer clear of potential conflicts of interest.

Don Ahern, President and CEO of Ahern Rentals. Chair of the Corrections, Parole and Probation Task Force. Don was a caring task force chair. He arranged and led a task force tour of the Nevada State Prison in Carson City. He developed and promoted possibly the most compelling and cost-effective long-term recommendation for Nevada's corrections system—moving its prisons closer to its population bases so that they can be supported economically.

Barbara Smith Campbell, Founder and CEO of Consensus LLC, former Vice President of Finance for MGM Grand Resorts Development and **former Chair of the Nevada Tax Commission**. Chair of Purchasing/Procurement Task Force. Barbara is one of very few individuals in Nevada who understands and can explain the state's complex tax system. That expertise was useful to the Commission and its deliberations. Barbara was an energetic chair of the Purchasing/Procurement Task Force, arranging meetings with state staff members so that issues were explored, explained and decided. She was the key drafter for the Sunset Committee recommendation adopted by the Commission.

R.B. "Bob" Feldman, President and CEO of Nevada General Insurance and Auto Insurance America, operating in three states. Chair of Department of Motor Vehicles and Public Employee Benefit Task Forces. He was instrumental in bringing DMV insurance and uninsured motorist issues to successful conclusions. His intimate knowledge of insurance matters also contributed to successful interactions between SAGE staff and PEBP administrators, which led to better mutual understandings and far more useful SAGE recommendations. Bob also acted as a liaison between SAGE staff and the Nevada Insurance Council.

Bob Forbuss, former President of Mercy Ambulance, now AMR, in Las Vegas. Chair of Mental Health Services Task Force. Bob was a faithful and attentive participant at SAGE Commission meetings.

Randy Garcia, founder and CEO of The Investment Counsel Company. Randy was an insightful critic of SAGE proposals and used his intellect and research capabilities to recommend many constructive revisions to improve them before they were adopted as SAGE recommendations.

David Goldwater, President of Goldwater Capital Nevada, LLC and **former Nevada State Assemblyman**. Chair of Budget Process Task Force. David made two very productive and complete power point presentations to the SAGE Commission on the budget process. His intimate knowledge of state government operations from the perspective of a former State Assemblyman led to insightful contributions to the Commission and its staff.

Steve Greathouse, former Senior Vice President of Operations for Mandalay Resort Group, former CEO of Alliance Gaming and **former President of Harrah's-Casino Hotel Division**. Chair of Health Care Systems Task Force. Steve was an active, effective task force chair. He was an articulate, diplomatic source of information about Nevada's gaming sector, an important factor in the Commission's understanding of this, the primary source of state revenues. He volunteered to help other Commissioners when needed.

Steve Hill, Senior Vice President of California Portland Cement, **founder and President of Silver State Materials**, now a subsidiary of California Portland Cement. Steve's role as Chairman of the Board of the Las Vegas Chamber of Commerce during his service on the Commission was the source of important contributions. Notably, he was able to provide access to and information regarding the Chamber's Fiscal Analysis Briefs on public and private sector compensation.

Jan Jones, Senior Vice President of Harrah's Entertainment, Internal and External Communications/Government Relations, **former two-term Mayor of Las Vegas**, and former Chairwoman of the Las Vegas Convention and Visitors Authority. Chair of Personnel Task Force. Jan's experience as Las Vegas Mayor provided the Commission with insights into the vagaries of local government in Nevada. As chair of the Personnel Task Force, she quickly culled through a long list of issues to attack those on which some progress seemed likely. She then organized stakeholder meetings in an attempt to achieve some consensus on them. She helped arrange a major Harrah's donation to SAGE.

Howard Putnam, former CEO of Southwest and Braniff Airlines, former Group Vice President for United Airlines, Author, Speaker and Business Advisor. Chair of Information Technology Task Force. Howard's performance as commissioner and task force chair was notable. His task force performed as originally contemplated, with regular, productive meetings, resulting in a total of five IT recommendations eventually approved by the full SAGE Commission. He was a ready resource at Commission meetings, willing and able to provide the perspective of a former CEO and current speaker on best business practices.

Jerome Snyder, industrial park developer, creator of Bingo Palace, later Station Casinos, Inc. and **owner of Sun West Bank and Integrated Financial Associates.** Chair of Real Estate Task Force. Jerry put a considerable amount of time and effort into developing potential real estate and public private partnership recommendations for the Commission and the Governor. Jerry consistently made himself available to staff for advice, support and whatever meetings might require his attendance.

Jim Thornton, founder and President of Nevada Paving, later sold to Granite Construction Company, **former Reno City Councilman**. Chair of Department of Transportation Task Force. Jim was a solid commissioner and an excellent chair for the NDOT task force. He arranged meetings with private sector contractors on the task force, NDOT senior staff and the Northern Nevada Association of General Contractors, while working with staff to help draft four NDOT proposals, which were approved by the Commission.

Carole Vilardo, President of Nevada Taxpayers Association (NTA). Chair of Health and Human Services Regulatory and Standardization Task Force. Carole was invaluable to the Commission as its on-site "institutional memory" at all Commission meetings. Her years as President of NTA meant there were few prior state government reform proposals of which she was unaware. She was of great assistance in staff research regarding prior NTA recommendations and provided access to relevant activities in other states across the US.

Each SAGE Commission member served entirely without compensation for eighteen months.

SAGE Commission Staff

Frank Partlow, Executive Director, **Brigadier General US Army, retired**, former Chief of Staff of the US Government Printing Office and founder of the Northern Nevada Network. Staff supervisor for the IT, Real Estate, Department of Corrections, PEBP, Purchasing and Procurement, and NDOT task forces.

Perry Comeaux, Deputy Director, **former Nevada State Budget Director**. Staff supervisor for all three Health and Human Services task forces as well as Budget Process and Personnel task forces. Perry's years as a national award winning State Budget Director were invaluable to the SAGE Commission and staff for all the obvious reasons, but his real value was as a true "insider" in state government. He knew where to look and who to talk to regarding virtually any issue. He quickly moved into borrowed space in the current State

Budget Director's offices, from which he was able to access valuable information on a timely basis, without going through any formal process. As a veteran of many legislatures, he was able and willing to guide staff through the 2009 session. His quiet, good-humored professionalism quickly infected all of us.

Suzanne Kilgore, General Manager, **former Executive Director, Custom Tailor and Designers Association**, Washington, DC. There were two absolutely indispensable folks involved with SAGE, Bruce James and Suzanne Kilgore. She was responsible for all SAGE business matters--maintaining its non profit charter and all of its finances from fund raising, through budgeting, payroll, contracting, banking and maintaining business relationships with the Community Foundation of Northern Nevada. She handled all aspects of meetings--agendas, open meeting law compliance, note taking, recording and production of minutes. She arranged all travel, wrote and distributed press releases, drafted 90-day reports to the Governor and maintained the SAGE web site. She reviewed, edited and formatted all SAGE recommendations and drafted the Grants Management proposal. We could not have survived without her cheerful, multi-tasking professionalism.

State Staff Support

Michael Willden, Director, Department of Health and Human Services. Michael and his administrators were ready for us. He knew what changes were required in HHS operations and was articulate and convincing in his presentations regarding these changes. It is no accident that seven of the first eight SAGE Recommendations involved Health and Human Services.

Daniel Stockwell, Director, Department of Information Technology and CIO. From the beginning, Dan volunteered his services to the Commission and its staff. He coordinated with the IT Task Force seamlessly, constantly providing quality information and insuring his senior staff's attendance at its meetings.

Leslie Johnstone, Executive Officer, Public Employee Benefits Program. Without Leslie's counsel and actuarial support, SAGE staff could not have written and evaluated its PEBP recommendations. It should be understood that she supported SAGE, but her loyalties properly remained with the PEBP Board.

Susan Martinovich, Director, Department of Transportation. Susan cooperated with the NDOT task force from the start. She and her staff provided the most complete and professional briefings we received. She was always available to work on recommendation details thereafter.

Greg Smith, Administrator, Purchasing Division. Greg and his staff demonstrated repeatedly that his division is on top of Nevada's purchasing and procurement functions—the reason there were no recommendations is this area.

Howard Skolnik, Corrections Director, Department of Corrections. Howard was available for meetings and consultations throughout the SAGE process. He worked closely with the Corrections Task Force, its chairman and senior advisor. He arranged and attended a first class tour of the Nevada State Prison.

Andrew Clinger, Director of Administration and Budget Director. Although swamped, dealing daily with the worst fiscal crisis in Nevada history, Andrew was always supportive with whatever information was required.

Edgar Roberts, Director, Department of Motor Vehicles. From the outset, Edgar and his staff made themselves fully available to SAGE staff and task force members and worked responsively to identify solutions on DMV issues.

Todd Rich, Director, Department of Personnel. Although Todd left this position while SAGE was still getting organized, he had provided an extensive, thoughtful briefing paper, which was still in use long after he departed.

Veronica Dahir, Associate Director and Kerry Kleyman Center for Research Design and Analysis, University of Nevada, Reno. Veronica supervised Kerry's design, conduct and analysis of the SAGE survey of state employees.

SAGE Senior Advisors

These recognized experts in their fields donated their time to SAGE Task Forces in their deliberations and drafting of proposals to present to the Commission.

IT Task Force:

Laura Schmidt, Department of Technology Services, Washoe County

Katherine C. Holland, General Manager and Vice President IBM Global Life Sciences

Mike Wash, Chief Information Officer, US Government Printing Office, Washington, DC

Corrections/Parole and Probation Task Force:

Bob Bayer, former Director, Nevada Department of Corrections, Adjunct Professor, University of Maryland and UNR

Health and Human Services Task Forces (Pharmaceutical Management):

Poonam Alaigh, MD, MSHCPM, FACP

Real Estate Task Force:

Jim Steinmann, Consultant

Chapter 10

Other Commission Discussion Topics

Commissioners met for months as members of task forces and in seventeen all day meetings of the full Commission. Many ideas were discussed which were discarded, either because they appeared to be outside the Commission's charter or they exceeded its research, financial or time resources. Of these, three stand out as having the potential for further examination, even though they were not investigated extensively by staff, nor addressed conclusively by the full Commission.

1. A **Nevada State Vision** should be agreed and updated periodically. If an entity doesn't know where it is going, any road will take it there. From a vision, goals, objectives, programs and performance measures can be derived and their outcomes can be measured.

2. **Effective performance measures** should be created and implemented for every program funded by the state. The goal is to be able to demonstrate whether adding resources to a particular program will actually improve expected outcomes. Such outcomes should be directly related to the agreed vision or a legislative intent. If improved outcomes cannot be proven through quantifiable measurements, how can it be argued that funding to any government program should be continued or increased?

3. **An interim 60-day Legislative Session** confined entirely to budget update issues should be mandated and implemented. The Interim Finance Committee (IFC) process has become a dysfunctional exercise in micromanagement, which is inconsistent with cost effective, efficient state government in this century. Meanwhile, two-year economic projections have proven to be impossible in the global economy in which Nevada government must now operate.

Chapter 11

A Grand Bargain

Voters and taxpayers affected by the "great recession" can see that one group of Americans has been practically unaffected by it—government employees at all levels. Their hours have been cut only marginally, they have gold plated benefits, and they are almost impossible to fire. In good times, few Nevadans notice these things. In bad times the disparity grates. Cops and firefighters retire in their 40's and draw defined benefits for life. Recently, the Reno City Council had to re-budget hundreds of thousands of dollars to buy 75 days of unused vacation time which each projected retiring firefighter was allowed by union contract to sell. Including benefits and overtime, some Nevada firefighters and police make more than their management, a few as much as $300,000 per year. Nevada's teachers union got its wish to raise room taxes across the state, but won't allow its members to be evaluated based on student performance, potentially costing the state millions of dollars in federal stimulus funds.

One should not overstate taxpayer rage. Most Nevadans justifiably admire teachers, police officers and firefighters. They like receiving government benefits, too, and are always in favor of taxing somebody else, like tourists, for the services they want. Roughly half of all Nevadans pay no federal income tax at all and, of course, none of them pay state income tax. ***The problem with all of this is that it is not sustainable.***

Unlike the federal government, Nevada is not allowed to print money to pay for the things its government and citizens think they are entitled to have. Something has to give. People don't like tradeoffs between children with no health care and public employee health care benefits, but those are the actual choices involved. Where the political leadership to make them will come from in Nevada is anybody's guess at this point.

Senator Bill Raggio reminds critics who allege that Nevada's spending has increased more than its population and inflation that such a situation has been contrary to Nevada statutes since the 1970's. Yet, the actual numbers document a real problem.

The Nevada Policy Research Institute has published US Census Bureau calculations showing that Nevada's tax revenues doubled between 2002 and 2007. During "those giddy days," its legislature showed no restraint, creating costly new programs without provision for the inevitable slow down. Total state government revenue grew by 106 percent, outpacing Nevada's population growth, as well as the national rate for increases in state government revenue. Basically, Nevada's part time lawmakers, particularly those elected each two years, use boom periods to pander to their constituents with costly new programs, then use economic downturns as an excuse to raise new taxes, as they did in 2003 and 2009, instead of cutting spending.

U.S. and Nevada labor statistics also provide some food for thought. In 1986, local and state government employee average earnings ranked sixth and seventh in Nevada at $22,419 and $21,574, respectively. By comparison Nevada mining employee earnings in 1986 were $30,863 and construction $24,294. By 2008, mining had jumped to $54,017 and construction to $49,753, first and third in Nevada. However, second place in 2008 was held by state government employees at $51,402, and fourth place by local government at $49,334.

Meanwhile, the search goes on for the "perfectly fair tax" and the "stable tax base." That 49 of the 50 US states are currently suffering fiscal crises of varying magnitudes, even though each of their "tax bases" is significantly different, does not seem to dissuade those participating in this search. Conversely, Knight Allen, a Las Vegas citizen, has provided the SAGE Commission with some brutal reminders:

- There is no such thing as a "stable" tax base. Every penny of revenue generated by a tax system must flow from the economic performance of a market economy. The dominant characteristic of a market economy is expansion and retraction, growth and recession. There is no tax system, especially in an open, global economy, which can mitigate, let alone control, these economic forces.

- A "broad based" tax system is oppressive and regressive because, by definition, it taxes the "basic necessities" of life.

- Corporations and businesses do not pay taxes. As Adam Smith first said: "profits of merchants are a subject not taxable directly...the final payment of all such taxes must fall, with considerable overcharge, upon the consumers."

Nevadans must understand that Las Vegas provides 75% of Nevada gaming related taxes and these make up 60% of the state's General Fund. Formerly believed by many to be "recession-proof," in this recession Las Vegas gaming related revenues have suffered double-digit declines, along with suffering through 15% unemployment and the highest real estate foreclosures in the nation. Any recovery in Las Vegas will necessarily follow the rest of the US, if and when consumers begin to feel comfortable with the sort of discretionary spending which "stays in Las Vegas."

Some experts think Las Vegas may never return to anything like its former profitability. Bankers, for example, have stopped lending and bankruptcies of the "General Motors" companies in the gaming industry are almost inevitable. Others more optimistically look to 2012 as the beginning of a recovery there. Regardless, there is no hope of any significant state General Fund recovery in Nevada in time to affect the 2011 legislative session and little hope of returning General Fund revenues even to 2007 levels by the 2013 session.

Diversifying Nevada's economy with "new, green energy industries," which will grow its jobs and fiscal revenues, are many years away. Given the fact that virtually every other economic entity in the world is competing with Nevada to generate these same green jobs and revenues, success here is problematic in any case. In the near term, we are stuck with SAGE-like approaches for better or for worse. Bargains and compromises usually involve both sides being equally unhappy. That, in a nutshell, is the only near term future available to Nevadans — equally shared unhappiness.

Hope for Nevada rests in some sort of "Grand Bargain" struck by moderates in the middle of Nevada's political spectrum between "no

new tax" Republicans and liberal Democrats, who are beholden to Nevada's public sector unions and a powerful legislative caucus. If Nevada is unable to elect enough reasonable, middle of the road legislators, who come to their responsibilities armed with some specific ideas
of how such an agreement could be achieved and implemented, its near
term future is bleak. Electioneering around slogans like "no new taxes,
its for the kids, or lock up the criminals" is as pointless as it will be unproductive. Candidates and voters must evaluate specific, distinct
spending cuts and reasonable avenues to enhance government revenues at all levels. The SAGE Commission's recommendations and
other ideas in this book are designed to help them to do just that.

The 2011 and 2013 legislatures could dither and deliberate away
119 of their 120 days, then take a meat ax to good government programs and employee jobs just as was done in 2009. For some Nevadans, that outcome would simply be a sad spectacle. For others, it would
be an unnecessary tragedy, which would likely affect the rest of their
lives — government employees, state benefit recipients, indigent children and many more. There are definitive ways to cut or eliminate
those government programs which cannot validate their current return
on investment. They may be harder to find but they are much easier to
live with and SAGE has pointed the way to many of them. There is no
need to dither. Turn over the potentially most productive of SAGE's 44
recommendations to the Legislative Counsel Bureau to run the numbers and review the statutes. That process can begin immediately,
given some good will and good sense during and after the 2010 political
season.

During my twenty years in Nevada, culminated by my twenty
months with the SAGE Commission, **I have developed my own version of a Grand Bargain**. I believe that in return for submitting to
new taxes, a new "tax structure" and other revenue enhancements **it
should include:**

• **Approving SAGE recommendations,** especially those on PEBP
  and PERS.

• **"Home rule"** for Nevada's cities and counties. The principle that
  governments which are closest to the people govern best should be

honored in fact as well as in rhetoric. A state legislature that is unable to balance its own budget without raiding the property taxes on which its cities and counties depend is not likely to be of much help to city councils and county commissions. I believe that potential consolidations within and among local governments could be particularly beneficial to Nevada's overlapping governmental jurisdictions in Clark and Washoe Counties, while saving significant tax dollars currently spent to finance duplicated local government services. However, for consolidation of functions or governments to be attractive fiscally, at least two major changes are required from the State Legislature.

First, **NRS 288 Public sector union negotiations** between local governments and their fire and police providers **should be conducted under Nevada's Open Meeting laws**. Exactly who is asking for what in new or revised labor contracts must be evident to taxpayers who are entitled to know where 75% of their local tax dollars are going and why. They are empowered to know by Nevada's Open Meeting laws. Full disclosure of this information must be made before any city council or county commission vote is taken to approve any contract.

Second, **NRS 280** should be revised to mandate that contract negotiations with consolidated public sector unions created to support consolidated public entities be conducted under this revised NRS 288. "Cherry picking" is a process whereby consolidated public sector union contracts include the contract provision or provisions most favorable to union members in each contracted area. **"Cherry picking"** between participating unions in a consolidated contract **should not be required by NRS 280**, as is currently the case. Under this statute, it is virtually impossible to save any significant amounts of taxpayer dollars through consolidation.

- Establishing an independent a task force to **scrutinize Nevada's system of higher education** to eliminate costly and superfluous programs and practices.

- Streamlining **Nevada K-12 education**, primarily by eliminating overhead, implementing merit pay in lieu of seniority and promoting proven innovative and entrepreneurial education techniques. The contention that simply spending more money on K-12 education will yield better results, like higher graduation rates, is not supported by reasonable analysis.

- Beginning an urgent investigation of **innovative new approaches to Yucca Mountain**, which moves from a concept of long term to interim storage, reprocessing spent fuel, running a high tech R&D center and collecting extensive federal compensation which is available to the state.

Public sector unions and their supporters should understand that the undeniable central cause of the bankruptcy of that icon of American industry, General Motors, was unsustainable pension and health care benefits extracted from the company over the years by the powerful United Auto Workers Union (UAW).

Yes, but public sector unions can't strike and governments can't declare bankruptcy. That is the past, not the present or the future. In 2008, the city council of Vallejo, California voted unanimously to declare bankruptcy rather than trying to continue to pay a police captain $306,000 per year or its firefighters an average of $171,000, with 21 of them making more than $200,000. Columnist George Will called this *an ominous portent for other cities and some states, few of which are accumulating financial resources sufficient to fulfill pension and benefit promises they have made to their employees.* A court agreed with Vallejo, requiring its unions (like the UAW with GM) to negotiate a "plan of adjustment." Bankruptcy has since spread from Vallejo to threaten the entire state of California.

Nevadans need to learn a crucial lesson from California and all the other states and local governments across the country which are struggling during this recession. Nevada's economy and fiscal resources are not going to grow their way out of the fiscal crises caused by this recession. ***The status quo in Nevada's state and local governments is simply unsustainable because the current systems for providing this level of government services in Nevada are unaffordable.***

12. Appendix

Final SAGE Commission Report to the Governor

Final Report

of the

Nevada Spending and Government Efficiency
(SAGE) Commission

to

Governor Jim Gibbons

January 7, 2010

Nevada SAGE Commission
Spending and Government Efficiency

Post Office Box 2700 ● Reno NV 89505
www.sagenevada.org

January 7, 2010

Governor
Jim Gibbons

Chairman
Bruce R. James

Commissioners

Don Ahern

Barbara S. Campbell

Robert B. Feldman

Robert Forbuss

Randy A. Garcia

David Goldwater

Stephen Greathouse

Steven D. Hill

Jan Jones

Howard Putnam

Jerome Snyder

Jim Thornton

Carole Vilardo

Staff
Executive Director
Frank A. Partlow
Deputy Director
J. Perry Comeaux
General Manager
Suzanne Kilgore

The Honorable Jim Gibbons
Office of the Governor
State of Nevada
101 N. Carson Street
Carson City, NV 89701

Dear Governor Gibbons,

On behalf of the Nevada Spending and Government Efficiency (SAGE) Commission I submit our final report to you together with our observations about the process and suggestions for the future.

Shortly after your election as Governor in November 2007 it became obvious that the State could no longer afford to continue government spending at the rate that our growing population and tax revenues had allowed in the previous decade. The rate of population growth had declined and the national economy seemed in danger of entering a recession which could affect state tax collections. From the beginning of your term you began to speak of the necessity of making our state government smaller and more efficient to avoid the prospect of raising taxes in a declining economy.

By early Spring of 2008 many people had made suggestions to you for streamlining the government; to help in evaluating these suggestions you began to explore the idea of bringing a group of senior business leaders together to give you their best advice on how you might reduce spending while improving needed citizen services.

That led to your establishing the SAGE Commission in May 2008. Many states over the years, including Nevada, had tried their hand at similar studies with mixed results. There were two important differences in how you went about setting up the Nevada SAGE Commission. First, you decided to seek guidance from legislative leaders of both parties regarding the composition of the Commission membership; that led to your selecting 14 senior business leaders with widely different backgrounds, 7 Republicans and 7 Democrats, 10 from the South, 4 from the North, none conflicted by doing business with the State. Second, you established a maximum term of two years for the Commission to complete its work but rather than wait for one end report, you instructed the Commission to deliver its recommendations to you every 90 days.

Continued

At the first meeting of the Commission on June 26, 2008 you asked members to set aside politics, their own personal biases and prejudices, and to focus on what was best for Nevada. It was a powerful charge—you asked for our best collective advice on how to make government more efficient and more responsive, irrespective of the politics involved.

That set the tone that led the Commission in researching, developing and sending to you 44 recommendations, all but two of which were fully supported by all members present at the vote. (The two recommendations forwarded to you without unanimous support were not split by party line or geography but by the conscience of members so voting). In all, it was a remarkable show of true bipartisanship by each and all of the Commissioners through months of committee meetings and 17 all-day meetings of the full Commission, which alternated between Las Vegas and Reno.

From the beginning, Commissioners recognized that 14 wise people sitting around a table could, by themselves, contribute little. Based on our respective years of leading organizations we knew that the answers to streamlining government laid mainly with the State's own employees and managers. So, as a starting step, we instructed our three person professional staff to work with the Department leaders reporting directly to you, to identify those opportunities for immediate cost savings. In general, there was exceptional cooperation which led to many of our early recommendations. As a follow-on step, we worked with the University of Nevada, Reno to develop and administer by email a survey of all identifiable Executive Branch employees, seeking their suggestions for improving citizen services and reducing costs. In particular, we were looking for patterns within agencies and throughout government. Again, the cooperation of employees in this effort was exceptional, with their insights leading the Commission to develop several recommendations.

Commissioners also recognized that we would benefit from reviewing not only previous studies of Nevada spending and possible efficiencies but also those of other states, as well as seeking guidance from experts throughout the country. We asked our professional staff to undertake these reviews and report their findings to us. A delegation of Commissioners and staff members traveled to Washington to seek input from federal agencies including the Government Accountability Office (GAO), the Office of Management and Budget (OMB), and the General Services Administration (GSA). Meeting with the top officials of these agencies to learn about best practices throughout the country proved quite fruitful as we began our work.

With limited resources and time we decided to organize our work horizontally and vertically while seeking ways to both streamline state government and increase revenues without adding to tax burdens. Horizontally, we looked at those services which cut across all agencies such as Information Technology. Vertically, we focused on the six agencies out of approximately 200 that account for nearly 70% of the state's (non-education) spending: Health and Human Services, Corrections, Motor Vehicles, Transportation, Business and Industry, and Public Safety.

Continued

To Governor Jim Gibbons, SAGE Commission Report Cover Letter, January 7, 2010 Page 3 of 3

To make certain that we were getting input from as many sources as possible we established several Task Forces, each focusing on a specific horizontal or vertical area, each composed of a Commissioner and outside experts, including state employees, and a SAGE staff member. The Task Forces conducted interviews and held meetings inviting interested parties to provide their viewpoints. At Commission meetings, which were all public, we invited interested parties and experts to comment on proposed recommendations. In all, hundreds of citizens, educators, state employees, public officials, labor leaders, business people, and subject matter experts contributed to the Commission's final recommendations.

While we realize that government is designed to change incrementally, we strongly believe that the recommendations we have made to you are practical and ripe for implementation now. Our recommendations could save the state hundreds of millions of dollars in the short run and billions over the next decade and have the potential to add tens of millions of dollars to state revenues without increasing taxes. Some you can implement on your own initiative, many require working with the State Legislature to fully implement. While the Commission wrapped up our official work in December, our members, to a person, stand ready to assist you and the Legislature in implementation.

We thank you for the honor of allowing us to serve our fellow citizens.

Sincerely,

Bruce R. James
Chairman

ADDITIONAL OBSERVATIONS AND COMMENTS

- In general, Nevada has a lean state government workforce that is paid salaries equal or above the private sector. However, benefits, including taxpayer contributions to retirement and health care programs, greatly exceed the private sector. By combining the two, the average state worker is paid considerably more than their private sector counterpart. This is unaffordable in the short run and unsustainable in the long run as many states are now experiencing. The sooner Nevada addresses this, and the sooner total government employee compensation is brought into parity with the private sector, the sooner the state will achieve a balanced budget allowing it to provide needed citizen services at desired levels. Dealing with this issue alone will save half of all the money contained in the Sage Commission's recommendations. This is not just a financial issue; it is one of fairness for all of our citizens.

- The state budgeting process is archaic and in need of revision. The process itself distracts everyone from agency personnel to members of the legislature from focusing on the big picture by being forced to deal with minutia. We realize that there is a difference in fiscal prudence between the private and public sectors, but the federal government and many other states do a much better job than Nevada. This is important because it lies at the heart of doing more with less, of being able to provide needed public services in the most efficient manner. We saw example after example of the same basic public services being provided by multiple agencies in a duplicative fashion without any coordination. This is due in large measure to the way budgets are made and reviewed. We make several recommendations in regard to improving the process with the key one being program budgeting.

- It's hard to imagine any organization of the size of our state government, other than government, trying to operate with 200 operating units or agencies. In the private sector we would consider such a structure unmanageable and a waste of valuable resources. However, in the private sector there is constant push for renewal and change to remain competitive. In the government sector it seems that once an entity or program is established it seldom goes away regardless of efficacy. The result is a waste of public resources. A million here, a million there, pretty soon it adds up to real money. Realizing that eliminating a state agency or commission or program faces the same obstacles that the federal government had a generation ago in trying to close obsolete military bases, the SAGE Commission recommended establishing the Nevada Sunset Commission to ensure periodic review of every state government entity and program to make certain it is still doing what it was established to do, is still necessary, and is cost efficient. If we had established such a commission a decade ago we would have far more resources today to provide critical citizen services.

- It is really necessary for the Nevada government to embrace a 21st century mentality in providing workplace tools for employees and in providing citizen services. It's not much of an exaggeration to say that the way the government is organized dates to the horse-and-buggy era. There are notable exceptions to this, but not many. It was beyond the ability of the SAGE Commission to address this other than collaterally. We strongly suggest that the state invest in establishing an overarching vision for providing effective, cost-efficient services using modern methods, and then hire appropriate consultants in each key area to help design and implement changes. Initially, the focus could be making investments with a payback of one year or less. But, it is important that each change build on the last, working toward a vision shared across state government.

ADDITIONAL OBSERVATIONS AND COMMENTS

- The State needs to address its real estate portfolio. The State not only does not have a real estate plan, it lacks a complete inventory, in one place, of its raw land, improved real estate, leased real estate, and water and mineral rights. The federal government and most other states have plans to sell obsolete holdings and to sell and lease back some facilities to raise cash and reduce carrying costs. In addition, many states are renegotiating leases to dramatically lower costs. The SAGE recommendation in this regard shows how this can be accomplished professionally and competitively with no out-of-pocket cost to the State.

- The lackadaisical attitude of public employees and officials throughout Nevada toward identifying and then relentlessly pursuing grant opportunities was puzzling to commissioners. Nevada rests last in receiving federal grant funds for which we are eligible. We have unnecessarily disadvantaged ourselves, leaving tens of millions of dollars on the table, by not having a strategic, managed focus on this opportunity as does almost every other state. This should be a full-out, statewide effort involving all jurisdictions eligible for such grants. (Yes, we heard the argument over and over that the state "does not have the required matching funds" which does not explain how 49 other states do it, or why we apply for only a fraction of available grants not requiring matching funds.) As a corollary, most foundations will not grant funds directly to a government entity for social services, but they will make grants to private sector, non-profit charities for services similar to or sometimes identical to what our government provides. Why not focus on partnerships with charities with such funding opportunities for the purpose of providing better and more cost effective services for our needy citizens?

- The SAGE Commission's mandate was to examine the Executive Branch of our government, excluding lower and higher education. Most good consultants would claim that they could suggest to any organization, public or private, ways to reduce operating costs by 10%. The SAGE Commission probably achieved similar results in terms of recommendations—without cost to taxpayers because the commission was privately funded by individuals and businesses. But, there is a big difference between recommending and enacting. Most members of the SAGE Commission are responsible in their own organizations for both creating a vision and leading others in its implementation. Here, we have to rely on others to grasp the vision behind each recommendation, embrace it themselves, and then enact it, all in a cauldron of various political calculations. SAGE commissioners have spent their time and money to provide our political leaders real, practical recommendations for reducing the costs of government. Just as SAGE commissioners did in their work, we hope our elected public officials can now set aside their partisan differences to put the public's interest first. If not now, when?

Recommendations
from the
Spending and Government Efficiency (SAGE) Commission
To Governor Jim Gibbons
June 1, 2008 through December 31, 2009

Note: The full text of all 44 SAGE Commission Recommendations can be found on the pages following.

1. Centralize billing for third party pay services in Mental Health and Developmental Services (MHDS). Explore data processing improvements and contracted billing services.

2. Staffing ratios in state operated psychiatric facilities need to be evaluated against private sector and national norms.

3. Implement Managed Care for the Aged, Blind and Disabled (ABD) groups in the Medicaid program in Clark and Washoe Counties, and expand Managed Care to women and children in four rural counties (Carson, Douglas, Lyon and Storey)

4. Acquire Distributive School Funding (DSA) for the Nevada Youth Training Center (NYTC) at Elko which is currently a high-school-like facility that is paid for with State general funds.

5. Complete the downsizing of the DMV night shift while maintaining the goal of a five-day title turnaround time.

6. Identify and coordinate the activities of all departments, agencies and institutions of the Executive Department that administer programs for the treatment of drug and alcohol abuse, or which provide funding to local governments for such programs.

7. Establish a program similar to the US Government Printing Office "GPO Express" schedules, providing steeply discounted digital printing, copying, finishing, delivery and other services by vendors on-line and at any of their outlets throughout the State, using access cards which document and bill all transactions electronically.

8. Examine ways to use the Indigent Accident Fund/Supplemental Relief Fund for federal matching funds to the Medicaid and Nevada Check Up programs.

9. Appoint a competent, disinterested third party to review the available options and recommend the most cost effective solution for the DMV auto insurance verification program to reduce the number of uninsured motorists currently driving illegally in Nevada to 10% or less.

10. Close the Nevada State Prison in Carson City immediately.

11. Evaluate a four-day work week for all non-essential Nevada State employees beginning October, 2009.

_____*end of First Report, September 30, 2008*

12. Over two years, beginning July 1, 2009, bring the State Public Employee Benefits Program (PEBP) health care subsidy for active Nevada employees and their dependents into approximate parity with those provided to their employees by Nevada private sector employers.

13. Modify retirement benefits for Public Employee Retirement System (PERS) members first employed on or after July 1, 2009.

14. Eliminate all State Public Employee Benefit Program (PEBP) subsidies for anyone who retires after July 1, 2009. Reduce existing subsidies for all plans for all currently retired State employees by twenty-five percent beginning July 1, 2009, and to a total reduction of fifty percent of existing subsidies beginning July 1, 2010. Eliminate all PEBP subsidies for all Medicare eligible retirees effective July 1, 2009.

15. Modify retirement benefits for all Public Employee Retirement System (PERS) members effective July 1, 2009, if legally permissible

16. The Senior Citizens Property Tax Assistance Program should be administered and fully funded by the various counties within the State of Nevada. The counties actually collect property tax with the majority of revenue being distributed to governmental entities within a county, so any rebate should be funded at that level.

17. Create a statutory Evaluation and Sunset Commission of not to exceed eleven members, three appointed by the governor, one from his administrative staff and two public members, and a total of eight appointed by majority and minority leaders of each house of the legislature from members of their respective bodies. This commission would make recommendations concerning statutorily created state agencies, boards and commissions regarding duplication of efforts, efficiencies to be achieved and potential elimination of functions. It would also recommend possible elimination, modification or continuance of all statutory tax exemptions, abatements and earmarks. The commission would present its findings to the Governor and Legislative Commission annually.

18. All state agencies should review the fees charged for services to ensure the fees cover the costs of providing the services. Fees and costs should be reviewed every two years

19. The State should conduct a detailed inventory of all State-owned real estate and buildings along with a portfolio optimization review of all leased facilities. An appointed task force should then evaluate the uses for all State owned property and appurtenant water rights, including Nevada System of Higher Education and NDOT real estate holdings, to determine the revenue producing potential of disposing of, leasing, trading, sale-leaseback or development opportunities by way of public/private partnerships. Such development might be financed by private equity and debt, tax exempt Certificates of Participation or other alternative means.

_____ *end of Second Report, December 31, 2008*

20. Design of a distance-based user fee pilot program by Nevada Department of Transportation (NDOT) and the Regional Transportation Commission (RTC) of Washoe County should be supported and funded now. A volunteer pilot program should be initiated in 2011, if feasible.

21. Provide State financial support to create a Nevada-oriented marketing and outreach program to supplement the national census advertising campaign.

22. Reinstate the requirement that Proof of Insurance from a licensed Nevada insurance company be presented to the Nevada Department of Motor Vehicles (DMV) for new vehicle registrations. Pursue programming on the DMV website to facilitate issuance of all temporary Proof of Insurance cards through the DMV website secure server.

23. Bulk copies of Driver Instruction booklets should be provided at a cost of $2 per booklet. License applicants who return for additional drive tests beyond the second try should be charged a duplicate fee in recognition of the additional personnel and administrative time and costs.

_____ *end of Third Report, March 31, 2009*

24. The State should make statutory changes to the interest rates paid on overpayment of taxes and charged on underpayment of taxes for both individuals and businesses. The State should adopt the index used by the Internal Revenue Service, as adjusted periodically, for businesses and individuals.

Recommendation #24 was adopted at the April 23, 2009 meeting as an interim Recommendation and sent to the Governor. It was also included in the June 30, 2009 Report.

25. Nevada's Department of Information Technology (DoIT) should implement and maintain an Enterprise Web Content Management System capable of hosting agency Web content and Web based applications, providing a single point of access for Nevada's citizens, while reducing costs.

26. Establish a common email platform for all Executive Branch Agencies.

_____ *end of Fourth Report, June 30, 2009*

27. Nevada should significantly improve its State level energy conservation efforts by enforcing its existing energy conservation plan and revising that plan consistent with 2009 organizational, financial, statutory and technical realities.

28. Request appointment of an Interim Legislative Committee to study the Public Works process.

29. Nevada Revised Statute (NRS) 408 regarding design-build contracts should be expanded to allow both an increased number of such projects per year and a significantly lower dollar threshold limit on such contracts.

30. In connection with SAGE Commission Recommendation #18 -- review of costs and fees -- included in the December 31, 2008 Report to the Governor, the following definitions should be adopted.

    Fee: A charge made to recover the cost of operating the program or providing the service, including indirect cost (overhead). A fee shall not be used for any purpose other than the actual direct and indirect cost of the program or service being provided to the end user.

    Cost: Direct cost of the program or service plus its allocable portion of indirect cost. Direct costs are those that can be identified specifically with a particular final cost objective. Indirect costs are those: (a) incurred for a joint or common purpose benefitting more than one cost objective; and (b) not readily assignable to the cost objectives specifically benefitted without effort disproportionate to the results achieved. (*from OMB Circular A-87*)

31. Authorize the Department of Corrections (DOC) to establish an intermediate sanction facility for certain probation violators and offenders, who are determined to be substance abusers. Substance abuse treatment is to be provided by the Department of Health and Human Services (HHS).

32. Nevada's information technology future should be defined through a comprehensive strategic planning process organized and developed by the State Information Technology Advisory Board (ITAB). Implementation of the resulting plan should be monitored, measured, and evaluated by a project manager separate from ITAB and the Department of Information Technology (DoIT).

33. Change the Interim Finance Committee (IFC) oversight thresholds as follows:

    A) Whenever a request for the revision of a work program of a department, institution or agency in an amount more than $50,000 would, when considered with all other changes in allotments for that work program, increase or decrease by 10 percent or $110,00, whichever is less, the expenditure level approved by the legislature. (NRS 353.220.4)

    B) For gifts and non-governmental grants exceeding $25,000 each and governmental grants exceeding $225,000 each and any grant that involves new employees. (NRS 353.335.5a and 5b)

    C) Specifically exclude revision of work program requests for balance forward funds and/or authority to the subsequent fiscal year where legislative authority exists and with no change in purpose; and de-augmentation of expenditure authority from any additional IFC approvals. (NRS 353.220.5 ADD 5d), d(i) and d(ii))

    D) The legislature shall review and adjust these amounts every six years. (NRS 353.220.5 ADD 5e).)

34. Revise language in NRS 242.131 so that State agencies, boards, and commissions in the Executive Department are not exempt from using Nevada Department of Information Technology (DoIT) professional services except for those infrastructures, enterprise architectures, facilities and personnel required for control of the specialized mission of the enterprise.

35. Solicit recommendations for a common telecommunications platform for all Executive branch State agencies and invite the Judicial and Legislative branches, Constitutional Officers, the Nevada System of Higher Education (NSHE), and cities and counties throughout the State to participate.

_____ *end of Fifth Report, September 30, 2009*

36. Explore the possibility of an exchange of Ely State Prison and Lovelock Correctional Center to companies that specialize in private corrections in return for construction of similar facilities located within existing large population centers to be determined by the Board of Prison Commissioners.

37. The Department of Corrections (DOC) should issue a request for proposals (RFP) to evaluate the costs and benefits of privatization of inmate medical and mental health care and the provision of pharmaceutical services.

38. Require directors of cabinet level departments to establish and implement cross training programs for their employees where feasible and practical, within a reasonable time. The goals of any such program should be to 1) help meet peak workloads and improve operational efficiency; 2) offer job enrichment opportunities; and 3) reduce costs by reducing use of outside contracts and/or overtime.

39. The Nevada Department of Transportation (NDOT) should perform a detailed analysis and review of all of the existing NDOT maintenance stations throughout the State with a view to eliminating some stations and consolidating others.

40. The Nevada Department of Transportation (NDOT) should commission a study of the costs and benefits associated with providing roadway maintenance by NDOT maintenance crews compared to outsourcing the same maintenance activities and develop decision factors for outsourcing such maintenance.

41. Create a communication structure, managed by a Nevada State Grants Coordinator, to facilitate dissemination of grant application opportunities and collaborative application efforts between agencies, county and local governments and non-profits, and identify a resource pool of experts and grant writers to support agencies in preparing applications. Create Grant Writer positions in selected state departments based on availability of grant opportunities.

42. Undertake a pilot project at one or more agencies to implement changes in Nevada's budget system. The pilot project should present, in the agencies selected, a program budget with clear performance evaluation criteria. The program budget should include funding in broad expenditure categories, as opposed to the three-part line item objects of expenditure, and measurable expected results at that level of funding should be included. The program budget can be presented with, or instead of, the traditional line item budget.

43. A method of establishing budget funding priorities based on different levels of expected revenues should be adopted.

44. Increase efforts to reduce costs for prescription drugs in the departments of Health and Human Services and Corrections by continuing ongoing programs and investigating new initiatives.

_____ *end of Sixth Report, December 31, 2009*

The full text of all 44 SAGE Commission Recommendations can be found on the pages following.

Recommendation #1

Centralize billing for third party pay services in Mental Health and Developmental Services (MHDS). Explore data processing improvements and contracted billing services.

Issue:
The long-standing MHDS approach to collecting third party payments for services using three independent regional offices (north, south, rural) with each office employing separate protocols is inefficient and results in lost revenue for the state.

<u>Start-Up Cost</u> Estimate: **unknown**

<u>Saving/Enhanced Revenue</u> Estimates: 1 Year: **$2.4 million***
                                        *net of start up cost estimate
                                        5 Year: **$12.0 million**

Explanation:
Historically, MHDS has collected third party payments for services in a decentralized manner. There are three separate regions (agencies) (north, south, rural) in the state.

By centralizing the MHDS billing/collections staff in one location (Carson City) MHDS can be more efficient and effective in collection efforts. MHDS has already begun this process and is transferring positions into the centralized unit. Proposed agency budgets for Fiscal Years 2010 and 2011 have been built with expected additional revenue from collections based on this change.

Additional revenue expected to be realized from centralizing the billing/collections staff is as follows:

Fiscal Year	North	South	Rural
FY10	$585,000	$1,775,000	$0.00
FY11	$615,000	$1,805,000	$0.00

Once initial consolidation of the billing function is accomplished, improvements to automated systems need to be explored for additional efficiencies. In addition, a detailed evaluation of using an outside contractor for billing services versus the state-operated billing services should be conducted.

Recommendation #2

**Staffing ratios in state operated psychiatric facilities
need to be evaluated against private sector and national norms.**

Issue:
Daily operating costs in the State's three psychiatric hospitals are
substantially higher than those in the private sector and in other states due in
large part to higher than normal staffing ratios. Although new facilities have
been built, staffing ratios have continued at the level required when facilities
were inefficient.

Start-Up Cost Estimate:	**None identified**
Saving/Enhanced Revenue Estimates: 1 Year:	**to be determined**
5-Year:	**to be determined**

Explanation
The State, through the Division of Mental Health and Developmental Services
(MHDS) and the Division of Child and Family Services (DCFS) operates three
psychiatric hospitals (2 adult, 1 children's) and one forensic facility. Daily
operating costs in these facilities are substantially higher than costs in some
private facilities and other states' publicly operated hospitals. Higher than
normal staffing ratios drive this cost significantly. Higher staffing ratios were
needed when the state utilized very inefficient, old hospitals built pre-1970.
Over the past ten years, the state has built and opened three new state-of-the-
art facilities which should allow for improved efficiencies.

Recommendation #3

Implement Managed Care for the Aged, Blind and Disabled (ABD) groups in the Medicaid program in Clark and Washoe Counties, and expand Managed Care to women and children in four rural counties (Carson, Douglas, Lyon and Storey).

Issue:
Managed Care, versus Fee-for-Service, is not currently mandated for the Aged, Blind and Disabled in any county or for women and children in any rural county. Expanding the Managed Care approach to these additional recipient groups would be a more cost effective means of providing these services to these populations.

<u>**Start-Up Cost**</u> **Estimate:**   **$225,000 - $425,000**

<u>**Saving/Enhanced Revenue**</u> **Estimates: 1 Year:**   **$7.3 million**

                                   5 Year: **$36.5 million**

Explanation:
The ABD Managed Care pilot project and Rural County expansion have both been suggested by the Department of HHS as options to save money. The ABD Managed Care plan was approved as a part of the 2007 Legislative Hearings. The Rural County expansion was suggested as a way to save money during the recent necessary budget reductions. Neither program has been implemented because of current economic conditions, and federal policy concerns which may require a waiver.

Expanding Managed Care to the Aged, Blind and Disabled (ABD) population was "priced" for the 2007 Legislative session (decision unit E400, BA3243). Start-up costs were identified as totaling $222,650 at that time. These costs included increased actuary services and increased quality review organization services. Estimated savings on switching ABD populations to Managed Care in 2007 were $2.7 million for year one and $13.5 million over five years.

On expanding managed care to rural counties for families/children, no estimate exists for start-up costs; however, the same issues noted above would apply on a smaller scale. If this change had been implemented for FY 2009, the savings over Fee-for-service costs were estimated at $4.6 million for the first year and $23 million over five years.

Estimated savings in the first year may be affected by the expected overlay of previous Fee-for-service costs not yet billed. When converting from a Fee-for-service plan to Managed Care plan, the State must expect to pay for "tail costs" (Fee-for-service bills which come in after the conversion) at the same time it would be paying fixed rates in the Managed Care program.

Recommendation #4

Acquire Distributive School Funding (DSA) for the Nevada Youth Training Center (NYTC) at Elko which is currently a high-school-like facility that is paid for with State general funds.

Issue:
The schools at the other Child and Family Services Division detention facilities are operated by the local school districts and funded through the DSA. The Division is currently in discussions with Elko County School District in an attempt to have the District take over the school. The Division also filed an application for a charter school, which would also result in DSA funding.

Start-Up Cost Estimate   **None**

Savings/Enhanced Revenue Estimates: 1 Year: **$455,000**

                                            5-Year: **$2.3 million**

Explanation:
The average number of youths detained at NYTC during a year has been between 150 and 160. This student "count" has not been included in the formula to determine guaranteed support through the DSA. Instead, a direct general fund appropriation has been made to Child and Family Services to operate the school.

The cost for fiscal year 2009 is budgeted at $1.4 million. This includes approximately $200,000 for a vocational education program that the Division will continue to operate. The remaining $1.2 million savings will be reduced by the cost of providing the guaranteed support per pupil, currently estimated at $5,323 per pupil.

The Child and Family Services Division estimates a reduced student count for future years of about 140 youths in the facility. This will result in a net savings to the general fund of about $455,000 per year.

Recommendation #5

Complete the downsizing of the DMV night shift while maintaining the goal of a five-day title turnaround time.

Issue:

Vehicle title processing improvements have allowed DMV to keep title turnaround time to within its goal of five days, allowing it to phase in transfer of two night shift FTEs into existing vacancies on the day shift, while maintaining the turnaround time goal.

Start-Up Cost Estimate:	**None**
Savings/Enhanced Revenue Estimates: 1 Year:	**$94,000**
5-Year:	**$470,000**

Explanation:

DMV currently processes over 400,000 title requests annually. In FY2002, DMV processed 343,000 title requests with a 14-day turnaround time. By FY 2008, 419,000 requests were processed in three days, in part due to a night shift supervisor and six technicians. Processing improvements will allow reductions in that staffing while maintaining the turnaround time goal, especially as a significant decrease in vehicle sales statewide has caused the number of requests to decline.

DMV will continue to monitor turnaround times, but expects that the goal can be maintained even when the economy rebounds.

Recommendation #6

Identify and coordinate the activities of all departments, agencies and institutions of the Executive Department that administer programs for the treatment of drug and alcohol abuse, or which provide funding to local governments for such programs.

Issue:

A report and recommendations on the subject matter of this recommendation mandated by Section 188.7 from Senate Bill 8 of the 20th Special Legislative Session to be submitted to the Governor by December 1, 2004, was never completed or submitted.

Start-Up Cost Estimate: **To be determined**

Savings/Enhanced Revenue Estimates: 1 Year: **Unknown**

                                                   5-Year: **Unknown**

Explanation:

Section 188.7 from Senate Bill 8 of the 20th Special Legislative Session directed that the Budget Division of the Department of Administration and the Fiscal Analysis Division of the Legislative Counsel Bureau jointly identify all departments, institutions and agencies of the Executive Department that administer programs for the treatment of drug and alcohol abuse, or which provide funding to local governments for such programs, and to develop a proposal for coordinating such programs to reduce the administrative costs associated with such programs and maximize the use of state revenues being expended for such programs.

This report with its recommendations was never completed and the coordination of such activities has not been implemented. The cost savings and maximization of the use of state revenues anticipated likewise have not yet been realized. This recommendation aims to achieve those ends.

Recommendation #7

Establish a program similar to the US Government Printing Office "GPO Express" schedules, providing steeply discounted digital printing, copying, finishing, delivery and other services by vendors on-line and at any of their outlets throughout the State, using access cards which document and bill all transactions electronically.

Issue:

State offices spend $2.5-$4.3 million on printing with the State Printing Unit and $5.6-$9.6 million with private vendors annually. Differences between State Printing Unit records and those provided by the State Budget Division on printing spending by State agencies suggest that printing purchases are charged to a variety of general ledger accounts. This discrepancy notwithstanding, a program like GPO Express should be established, where the State would specify and publish a price list for digital printing and related services, similar to the FedEx Office GPO Express schedule, specifying ordering and payment methodologies and terms, and contracting with any digital printer in the State willing to accept those terms. Such a system would result in significant savings for printing and shipping costs of digitally printed matter for taxpayer supported government agencies throughout the State, while continuing the State Printing Unit option for agency digital printing jobs which are more conveniently or more economically done by the State Printing Unit.

Start-Up Cost Estimate:	**None**
Savings/Enhanced Revenue Estimates: 1 Year:	**$700,000**
5-Year:	**$3.5 million**

Explanation:

The State Administrative Manual provides that all State printing and binding be done on a competitive basis and further advises that it is in the best interest of the State to do business with the State Printing Unit, "whenever possible." Sixty-six percent of that Unit's current business supports State executive branch agencies, 25%, the legislative branch, 6%, cities and counties and 3%, the judicial branch.

The US Government Printing Office (GPO) has established a "GPO Express" system of schedules with FedEx Office, providing savings on advertised pricing for digital printing, copying, finishing, delivery and other services. These services are provided to US Government agencies on line and at any of its 1500 outlets anywhere in the United States, using individual access cards, which document and bill all transactions electronically to the GPO.

Recent meetings with FedEx Office officials confirm corporate interest in providing this same sort of contractual arrangement with the State of Nevada. The State could also elect to offer FedEx Office schedules to any qualified digital printer in the State under similar terms and conditions as provided by the GPO Express contract. Government agencies typically are seeking convenience and rapid turnaround on digital print orders, which means they often pay retail premiums for such work. Since many State agency offices are not located in convenient proximity to the State Printing Unit, such statewide digital printing arrangements would not only cost far less, they would increase productivity, as well.

Recommendation #8

Examine ways to use the Indigent Accident Fund/Supplemental Relief Fund for federal matching funds to the Medicaid and Nevada Check Up programs.

Issue:
The state is disregarding $25-50 million dollars per year in federal matching funds for the Medicaid and Nevada Check Up programs because of legislative restrictions on application of the Indigent Accident Fund and the Supplemental Relief Fund.

Start-Up Cost Estimate: **Unknown**

Saving/Enhanced Revenue Estimates: 1 Year: **$25 - $50 million**

                                    5 Year: $125 - $250 million

Explanation:
Property tax rates include 2.5¢ per $100 to support medical care for indigent (poor) individuals who experience automobile accidents or catastrophic (over $25,000 health care) events. This creates approximately $25 million per year in the Indigent Accident Fund and Supplemental Income Fund (IAF/SAF).

Currently, no federal matching funds are obtained for this revenue, with the exception of a very small amount used to support a waiver (HIFA) in the Medicaid program to provide health care to pregnant women and low-income employees in small businesses.

If the state law directing how IAF/SAF funds can be expended was changed to allow for reimbursement of care provided to Medicaid eligible individuals and Nevada Check Up eligible children, then these funds would become eligible for Federal matching. The federal matching rate in the Medicaid program is 50% state/50% federal. The federal matching rate in the Check Up Program (children) is approximately 34% state/66% federal. This would result in an additional $25million to $50 million per year in reimbursement money available for county hospitals.

It is estimated that the Nevada Check Up program alone could use the entire additional amount generated from federal matching funds. In addressing this legislative change, care should be taken to ensure that the resulting increase in funds continues to be directed to the current recipients of IAF/Supplemental funds, namely hospitals and counties. At the very least, they should be protected from any decrease in current fund levels.

Recommendation #9

Appoint a competent, disinterested third party to review the available options and recommend the most cost effective solution for the DMV auto insurance verification program to reduce the number of uninsured motorists currently driving illegally in Nevada to 10% or less.

Issue:

Private vendors and insurance industry executives believe that for start up costs of $1 million and $700,000 annually, they can achieve a reduction of at least ten percent in Nevada's current 17-19% uninsured motorist population, beginning in 2009. DMV leadership prefers to do this work using its existing workforce to completely rewrite its insurance verification software by January 2010, at a cost of $387,000 and 23 FTE to operate the system after that.

Start-Up Cost Estimate:	**unknown**
Savings/Enhanced Revenue Estimates: 1 Year:	**$3.5 million**
5-Year:	**$20.9 million**

Explanation:

Nevada currently has 17-19% of its motorists driving uninsured motor vehicles. It is estimated that by cutting the uninsured population by 10%, the approximately 180,000 additional insured vehicles would generate $3.8 million annually in additional 3.5% insurance premium tax revenues.

On September 9, the Interim Finance Committee approved $387,000 for the DMV to design and develop what DMV characterizes as "modifications to the insurance program" in-house. Of the funding approved, $106,736 is for IT overtime hours and $266,490 for contract programmer hours. They intend to commence this work in January 2009, and estimate completion one year later.

Insurers characterize the work required as "a complete rewrite of the insurance verification software." They currently report to DMV using outdated magnetic tapes and disks, while DMV uses 20 FTEs to resolve the resultant insurance issues by telephone, because it has no upload, download or email communication capacity to generate prompt, accurate enforcement and collection actions. Utah, Texas, Florida, Wyoming, New Mexico and Colorado have successfully hired outside vendors, some of whom have over 10 years' experience in this field, to resolve similar uninsured motorist issues.

At an initial cost of $1 million and $700,000 annually thereafter, or about 50 cents per vehicle, Nevada could generate sufficient previously unpaid tax revenues to offset the costs of these contracts and cut its DMV workforce by up to 23 enforcement FTEs, as well.

Recommendation #10

Close the Nevada State Prison in Carson City immediately.

Issue:
Established in 1862, the Nevada State Prison in Carson City is one of the oldest prisons still operating in the United States at a cost to the state of $19 million annually. In addition, there exists a 104-page list of capital improvements required to bring this facility up to code at a cost estimated at between 40 and 50 million dollars.

Start-Up Cost Estimate:	**To be determined**
Savings/Enhanced Revenue Estimates: 1 Year:	**$19 million**
5-Year:	**$140 million**

Explanation:
A maximum security facility until 1989, this Nevada State Prison currently houses medium security inmates who are employed in a variety of work assignments, including the State License Plate factory. Design capacity of the facility is 591, but it currently houses 905 inmates. It has a total staff of 211. Both inmates and staff could be accommodated in other facilities throughout the State. The prison has serious current problems with both water and sewage. Lines of sight available in the facility require more staff per inmate than in newer facilities. There have been discussions and attempts to close the facility for at least ten years largely because of its poor condition and the mounting costs of upkeep.

An alternative to full closure is a partial closure by reopening the upper yard (units 6-13) and bringing it into the perimeter of the adjacent Warms Springs Correctional Center after certain capital improvements are completed at that facility. This alternative involves the expense of a new perimeter fence for the resulting institution and maintaining retained portions of a very old facility at a time of constrained state resources. However, the license plate plant and other prison industries which are located in the upper yard could then be retained, using inmates from Warm Springs in the interim by requiring Prison Industries pay for an officer to move them as required, and for the necessary utilities to keep these operations functioning.

Recommendation #11

Evaluate a four-day work week for all non-critical Nevada State employees beginning October, 2009.

Issue:
The state could realize significant potential savings in operation of state-owned buildings, reductions in vehicle emissions and enhanced State employee morale by providing all non-essential Nevada State services during four, ten-hour days per week, Monday-Thursday, instead of the current five, eight-hour days per week, Monday-Friday.

Start-Up Cost Estimate:	**To be determined**
Savings/Enhanced Revenue Estimates: 1 Year:	**$10 million**
5-Year:	**$50 million**

Explanation:
On August 4, 2008, the State of Utah began a one-year pilot program of four, 10-hour shifts, Monday-Thursday, for all State agencies. Agency managers have the discretion to schedule staff, but Utah's standard business hours will be 7:00 am-6:00 pm, Monday-Thursday. Public universities, the State court system, prisons and other critical services are exempt. This program will remain in effect for one year, until August, 2009, when the program will be evaluated and a determination made regarding continuing or terminating the program.

Utah expects to save significant monetary resources with this program, primarily in building operational costs and by spreading the load on its transportation infrastructure, while reducing energy use and resulting CO_2 emissions. Its initial estimates of cost savings were $14 million, with about 17,000 of its employees estimated to be affected by the new working hours. These estimates will be replaced by actual data, beginning January, 2009. The State also expects to improve provision of services to its citizens by extending them beyond the traditional hours of the workday. Utah officials also believe it will improve the quality of life of its employees and increase its ability to attract new talent into State government.

This recommendation anticipates that Nevada would effect the necessary legislative and executive authorizations to begin immediately to work with its neighbor in Utah to follow these evaluations of both the cost and non-monetary impacts of Utah's experiment with an altered work week. It anticipates that by October, 2009, or shortly thereafter, Nevada could make a fully informed decision to commence its own experimentation with an altered work week, based on its own independent evaluations of Utah's pilot program. Costs and savings estimates in this recommendation are based on about 15,000 State employees being impacted in any Nevada pilot program.

Although most states have an optional four-day work week option for their employees, Utah is the first to try a mandatory four-day work week. Such programs are fairly common among city and county governments nationwide, including Henderson and North Las Vegas, NV, and are becoming more so due to higher fuel prices and the overall fiscal pressures facing governments at all levels across the country.

Recommendation #12

Over two years, beginning July 1, 2009, bring the State Public Employee Benefits Program (PEBP) health care subsidy for active Nevada employees and their dependents into approximate parity with those provided to their employees by Nevada private sector employers.

Issue:
The cost of health insurance is shared between employer and employee in most public and private sector enterprises. Nevada's employee health care subsidies are established by the Legislature each biennium. They have exceeded those of some Nevada private sector employers and those in some other states. To establish fairness and promote competitiveness between Nevada's public and private sectors, these subsidies should be adjusted every two years based on a statistically valid survey of private sector employer health care subsidy practices.

Start-Up Cost Estimate:	**Undetermined**
Savings/Enhanced Revenue Estimates: 1 Year:	**$20.2 Million**
5-Year:	**$322.7 Million**

Explanation:
Over 26,000 active State employees and their dependents currently participate in some form of State PEBP health care insurance. These plans offer a variety of choices to employees and include benefits similar to those offered by Nevada's private sector employers The difference is that over a number of years, private sector employees have apparently been absorbing an increasing part of the cost of health insurance while the current State share of these costs is 95-100% for active employees and 85% for their dependents. The result is that a State employee's average monthly contribution for health insurance in 2009 is zero to $28 and between $62 and $194 for dependent coverage for a family of four. An employee of a major Las Vegas employer in 2009 will pay $104 and $323 for approximately the same insurance. This proposal envisions establishing State subsidies based on valid comparisons to those paid by Nevada's private sector employers of over 100 employees to determine a mean average private sector subsidy for all types of health insurance. State subsidies would then be brought to within five percent of this mean in two steps, on July 1, 2009 and July 1, 2010, to cushion the impact on State employees. State employee subsidies would be adjusted up or down each two years based on subsequent surveys of private sector employers. PEBP staff could also establish a base salary threshold below which the maximum employee share paid for active employee coverage and for dependent coverage would be fixed at specific percentages of the actual cost of the coverage.

The cost factors shown provide an illustrative example of the impact on the State's fiscal situation of subsidy reductions expected from this recommendation.

Recommendation #13

Modify retirement benefits for Public Employee Retirement System (PERS) members first employed on or after July 1, 2009.

Issue:
The cost of the PERS as it currently exists represents a significant financial obligation to both state and local governments in Nevada. The cost of fully funding that system is currently estimated to be $6.3 billion. That cost can be reduced while maintaining an acceptable level of retirement security for Nevada's public employees hired on or after July 1, 2009.

Start-Up Cost Estimate: **None Identified**

Savings/Enhanced Revenue Estimate: 5-Year: Approximately $100 Million

Explanation:
The proposed retirement plan modifications are as follows, and would apply prospectively to all employees hired on or after July 1, 2009:

1. Redefine "compensation" for purposes of benefit calculations to base pay only.
2. Change final average salary definition from average of three consecutive highest years to average of five consecutive highest years.
3. Establish compensation cap at 10% per year for five consecutive highest years for purposes of benefit calculation only.
4. The cost of purchasing years of service should be reviewed every biennium and priced to cover the full actuarial cost of the benefits purchased.
5. Impose a moratorium on PERS benefit enhancements until the plan is actuarially fully funded for three consecutive years and can continue to be actuarially fully funded; and sunset any enhancements so approved in ten years.
6. Eliminate retirement at any age with prescribed number of years of service and establish a minimum retirement age of 60. A reduced benefit would be paid at any age after 35 years of service.
7. Reduce the retirement multiplier from the current 2.67 to 2.15.

Items 6 and 7 should not be applied to police and fire members. That issue should be studied separately.

In addition, the Governor or Legislature should conduct an interim study and make recommendations to the 2011 Legislature for additional changes to the system, if appropriate.

Recommendation #14

Eliminate all State Public Employee Benefit Program (PEBP) subsidies for anyone who retires after July 1, 2009. Reduce existing subsidies for all plans for all currently retired State employees by twenty-five percent beginning July 1, 2009, and to a total reduction of fifty percent of existing subsidies beginning July 1, 2010. Eliminate all PEBP subsidies for all Medicare eligible retirees effective July 1, 2009.

Issue:
Nevada's employee health care subsidies are established by the Legislature each biennium. Over 7,800 retirees currently participate in some form of State PEBP health care insurance. This number is expected to rise to 8,200 by 2011, and rapidly increase thereafter, as over 43 percent of current State employees are eligible to retire within 10 years. Unlike retirees from most private sector employment and many states, Nevada retirees currently receive generous PEBP health care subsidies.

Start-Up Cost Estimate:		**None**
Savings/Enhanced Revenue Estimates: 1 Year:		**$23.6 Million**
	5-Year:	**$156.8 Million**

Explanation:
This proposal would eliminate all State PEBP subsidies for anyone who retires after July 1, 2009. These retirees would remain eligible to participate in PEBP, but would pay 100 percent of benefit costs. This proposal also envisages reducing State PEBP subsidies by twenty-five percent for all current retirees who are not eligible for Medicare, beginning on July 1, 2009, and to a total reduction of fifty percent of existing subsidies beginning July 1, 2010. Currently, these subsidies range between $356 and $696 per month at a cost to the State of $40 million per year. The expectation is that elimination of this subsidy will cause some retirement eligible State employees to retire before July 1, 2009, in order to qualify for this reduced subsidy. PEBP staff could also establish a retiree pension threshold below which the maximum retiree share paid for retiree coverage and for dependent coverage would be fixed at specific percentages of the actual cost of the coverage.

The existing $4 billion deficit required to fully fund the PEBP system for 30 years will be reduced during each year that these subsidy reductions are in effect.

Recommendation #15

Modify retirement benefits for all Public Employee Retirement System (PERS) members effective July 1, 2009, if legally permissible.

Issue:
The cost of the PERS as it currently exists represents a significant financial obligation to both state and local governments in Nevada. The cost of fully funding that system is currently estimated to be $6.3 billion. That cost can be reduced while maintaining an acceptable level of retirement security for Nevada's public employees.

Start-Up Cost Estimate: **None Identified**
Savings/Enhanced Revenue Estimate: *No estimates are available at this time. The savings estimates require actuarial calculations that can be   performed by the PERS actuarial consultants, if the PERS Board directs.*

Explanation:
The proposed retirement plan modifications are as follows, and would apply to all PERS members, if legally permissible:

1. The cost of purchasing years of service should be reviewed every biennium and priced to cover the full actuarial cost of the benefits purchased.
2. Impose a moratorium on PERS benefit enhancements until the plan is actuarially fully funded for three consecutive years and can continue to be actuarially fully funded, and sunset any enhancements so approved in ten years.

In addition, the Governor or Legislature should conduct an interim study and make recommendations to the 2011 Legislature for additional changes to the system, if appropriate.

Recommendation #16

The Senior Citizens Property Tax Assistance Program should be administered and fully funded by the various counties within the State of Nevada. The counties actually collect property tax with the majority of revenue being distributed to governmental entities within a county, so any rebate should be funded at that level.

<u>Issue:</u>
Although property taxes throughout the State are assessed and collected by counties, the Senior Citizens' Property Tax Rebate Program is currently administered by the State Department of Health and Human Services and the rebates to over 14,000 eligible home-owners and renters are paid from State General Fund revenues. This program was origi-nally created by the 1973 Legislature. This was done in response to an interim study con-ducted by the Legislative Commission and published in December 1972. The title of the study is "Senior Citizens Tax Relief Study" and the findings included the following: 1) Many senior citizens of this state are carrying an excessive property tax burden, which is disproportionate to their relatively fixed and limited income; 2) To lessen this burden, tax assistance legislation should be enacted; and 11) The program of assistance should be fi-nanced by the State.

Finding 11 was probably made because at that time the state was a major direct recipient of property tax revenue. Since that changed as a result of the so-called tax shift in the early 1980s, the funding of the program should be changed.

<u>Start-Up Cost</u> Estimate:	**Unknown**
<u>Savings/Enhanced Revenue</u> Estimates: 1-Year:	**$5,900,000**
5-Year:	**$30,000,000**

<u>Explanation:</u>
The Nevada Association of Counties, along with Clark and Washoe Counties, are on record as opposing transfer of the fiscal responsibility for this program to the State's county governments. There is less opposition to accepting responsibility for its admini-stration only. However, the State's counties assess and collect all property taxes through-out the State under existing law. Only seventeen cents per one hundred dollars assessed valuation of those collected property taxes are provided to the State. These State funds are reserved entirely to provide bonding capacity for the State's Capital Improvements Programs and administration of those programs by the State Public Works Board. None of this money is currently available to "refund" property taxes to eligible senior citizens. Meanwhile, Washoe County's general fund, for example, is allocated over $1.30 per hun-dred dollars assessed valuation collected from County property owners. Some of that money is collected from the same senior citizens who are eligible to receive rebates and some is collected from the landlords of senior citizen renters who are similarly eligible for rebates. Paying such rebates from State General Fund revenues, administered by State Health and Human Services Department employees, also paid by State General Fund reve-nues, is anachronistic at best and should be revised to reflect current fiscal and administra-tive realities.

Recommendation #17

Create a statutory Evaluation and Sunset Commission of not to exceed eleven members, three appointed by the governor, one from his administrative staff and two public members, and a total of eight appointed by majority and minority leaders of each house of the legislature from members of their respective bodies. This commission would make recommendations concerning statutorily created state agencies, boards and commissions regarding duplication of efforts, efficiencies to be achieved and potential elimination of functions. It would also recommend possible elimination, modification or continuance of all statutory tax exemptions, abatements and earmarks. The commission would present its findings to the Governor and Legislative Commission annually.

Issue:
While standard legislative oversight is concerned with agency or commission compliance with legislative policies, Sunset asks a more basic question: Do the agency's functions and statutory tax exemptions, tax abatements or tax earmarks continue to be needed? This proposal would create a unique opportunity for the Governor and Legislature to look closely at each agency, commission or board and make fundamental changes to an agency's, commission's or board's mission or operations if needed. In addition, it offers the opportunity for a planned review to determine the appropriateness of statutory tax exemptions, tax abatement or tax earmarks.

Start-Up Cost Estimate: **Unknown**
Savings/Enhanced Revenue Estimate: **Unknown**

Explanation:
Sunset is the regular assessment of the need for any non-constitutionally mandated state agencies, commissions, statutory tax exemptions, tax abatements or earmarks to exist. The State needs a formal process and structure to review on a rotating basis every 10 years the requirement for, as well as the policies and programs of, those state agencies and commissions not created by the constitution; to find duplication of other public services or programs; to improve each agency's operations and activities; to examine all statutory tax exemptions, tax abatements and tax earmarks and to evaluate the economic, financial and environmental benefits associated with these public policies. In most cases, agencies, commissions, tax exemptions, tax abatements and tax earmarks under Sunset review are automatically abolished unless legislation is enacted to continue them. The commission would schedule, not less than every 10 years, a review of state agencies, boards and commissions to review activities in accordance with their mission and/or purpose; for duplication with other public services and programs; and for potential ways to improve or modify their operations. The Commission would seek public input through hearings on every agency or commission and every statutory tax exemption, tax abatement or earmark under Sunset review and recommend actions on each to the full Legislature. While there is no precise way to estimate Commission expenditures, savings or enhanced revenues to be achieved in Nevada through this proposal, the comparable Texas Sunset Commission experience over 25 years there has yielded significant revenue savings through the process.

Recommendation #18

All state agencies should review the fees charged for services to ensure the fees cover the costs of providing the services. Fees and costs should be reviewed every two years.

Issue:
There are agency budget accounts for programs that provide services that contain General Fund appropriations as well as authority to receive fees from those to whom the services are provided.

Start-Up Cost Estimate:	**None**
Savings/Enhanced Revenue Estimate: 1-Year	**$1 Million+**
5-Year	**$5 Million+**

Explanation:
    An example of this is Consumer Health Protection within the Health Division of Health & Human Services, which provides regulatory services for areas such as radiological devices (x-ray machines), food establishment inspections and permitting, solid waste disposal, and so on. For Fiscal 2009 this program has a General Fund appropriation of $1.077 million. Fee income to this program is $1.632 million. Therefore, the general public is funding over a third of the cost of services provided to a specific segment of the community.
    Fees established to cover the actual costs of the services provided by other programs are also, in many cases, inadequate. This results in all taxpayers funding part of the cost of a service provided to a very small segment of the community. Unless public policy dictates otherwise, fees should be set to cover the actual cost of the service.
    Fees should not exceed the actual cost of the service, including reasonable administrative expenses. If fees produce excess revenue, the amount of the fees should be reduced rather than used for other governmental purposes.

Recommendation #19

The State should conduct a detailed inventory of all State-owned real estate and buildings along with a portfolio optimization review of all leased facilities. An appointed task force should then evaluate the uses for all State owned property and appurtenant water rights, including Nevada System of Higher Education and NDOT real estate holdings, to determine the revenue producing potential of disposing of, leasing, trading, sale-leaseback or development opportunities by way of public/private partnerships. Such development might be financed by private equity and debt, tax exempt Certificates of Participation or other alternative means.

Issue:
The State owns surplus real estate that has been acquired for right of way, project expansion or held as a result of previous transactions. The State also leases 1.5 million square feet of space in 212 leases at an annual cost of $28 million. While the State owns and operates multiple developed real estate properties through various agencies, State real estate operations are now managed by separate entities, including the Public Works Board, Buildings and Grounds and State Lands Divisions, along with others both in and outside the Executive Branch.

Start-Up Cost Estimate: **None Identified**
Savings/Enhanced Revenue Estimate: **Available upon completion of Inventory**

Explanation:
The US Office of Management and Budget recommends conducting a detailed review of State-owned real property to distinguish performing from non-performing real estate assets. To date, a minimum of fifteen states has conducted such reviews. The results of such review and subsequent implementation of a well conceived real estate strategy can include elimination of unneeded assets consistent with their current market value, improving the condition of mission critical assets, management of mission critical assets at appropriate costs and maximum utilization of retained real property. Under-utilized properties can be disposed of by lease, sale, sale-leaseback or used in trade with private sector developers for public private partnership on other sites and/or incorporation of assets not essential for State ownership but proper for State use. Potential income from such operations is millions of dollars.

Nevada has a good start on assembling this inventory with data available from the State Lands Division and from the Capitol Complex and Las Vegas Master Plans prepared in 2002 and 2005, respectively. It is now appropriate to

Recommendation #19, *continued*

Explanation, *continued*

add vacant property and to perform a comprehensive analysis of State leased space to consolidate operations, eliminate redundancies and inefficiencies and to take advantage of State purchasing power and current market conditions. Annual holding costs, potential revenues available through sale, trade, lease, or development should be identified and specific recommendations provided to the 2011 Legislature, pursuant to appropriate authorizations by the 2009 Legislature.

Private sector consultants assisted the State with previous master planning efforts and should be considered for these activities as well, because the State does not have sufficient internal resources to conduct these inventories and evaluations. The State of Virginia, for example, engaged a nationally known commercial real estate company for an operational review of its real property assets, involving 520,000 acres of land, 11,000 owned buildings and 1,350 active leases. The developed plan focused on consolidating and co-locating agencies into owned and long term leased facilities. It consolidated real estate authority under a single organization responsible for providing and managing all space to all state agencies, allowing Virginia to leverage its buying power as landlord and tenant. Improved and more cost effective facilities management services levels were included and estimated savings over ten years from these recommendations were $70 million. Such companies may be willing to perform similar services for Nevada for minimal up front costs through contract arrangements which include fee schedules for the sale or lease of any State real estate assets consistent with identified State needs.

Recommendation #20

Design of a distance-based user fee pilot program by Nevada Department of Transportation (NDOT) and the Regional Transportation Commission (RTC) of Washoe County should be supported and funded now. A volunteer pilot program should be initiated in 2011, if feasible.

Issue:
Construction and maintenance of highways and local roads in Nevada are financed mainly by federal and state fuel taxes, which currently total 53 cents per gallon and have not been raised since 1992. Meanwhile, users are travelling more per capita on Nevada's highways, while they are paying for less fuel per capita due to increased fuel efficiency. As the future of Nevada and the nation move towards alternative energy sources for oil independence and the fight against global warming, the fuel tax model will eventually need to be replaced if the highway system is to remain viable.

Start-Up Cost Estimate:	**$250,000**
Savings/Enhanced Revenue Estimates: 1-Year:	**Unknown**
5-Year:	**Unknown**

Explanation:
Whether by reduction in supply, increased fuel efficiency or excessive cost of gasoline and diesel, the fuel tax will become a less reliable source of highway revenue in the future. Consequently, NDOT and the Washoe RTC have collaborated to begin a process to change Nevada's highway revenue transportation model. The development of a pilot project to test this model will take about 16 months and will be funded jointly by NDOT and the RTC, using transportation funding available to each. Issues which the study will need to address include available technologies, fee structure, potential partners, funding sources, public support and potential privacy concerns. The project is sup-ported by the University of Nevada which will develop a pilot program protocol which could be implemented over a twelve-month period beginning as soon as the fall of 2011 at a currently estimated cost of $5 million, the funding of which is to be determined.

There are two primary variables which affect construction, maintenance and operational costs of highways: travel demand and structural demand. Travel demand consists of the number and type of vehicles on the roads. When demand exceeds capacity, congestion results. To avoid new road construction, demand can be spread through-out the day, avoiding peak travel periods. Structural demand is based on the number and weight of vehicles. This distance-based user fee program will seek to address both of these variables. In addition, a major consideration that will be addressed are the privacy concerns and development of privacy protocols necessary to protect the public's interests.

Europeans and some US states have experimented successfully with these new user fees. Oregon DOT's 2006, 12-month pilot program concluded that a mileage fee program is viable using on-vehicle devices and existing technologies, with 91 percent of participants supporting the program and privacy protection possible using certain technologies.

Recommendation #21

Provide State financial support to create a Nevada-oriented marketing and outreach program to supplement the national census advertising campaign.

Issue:
According to the Census Bureau, over $3 trillion in funding is allocated nationwide based on Census figures. In 2000, the Legislative Counsel Bureau estimated that the state lost $670 per person per year for every Nevadan missed by the 2000 Census. Recently, the Legislative Counsel Bureau, Nevada State Data Center, and Nevada State Demographer came together to update that figure for 2010. Due to the combined effects of inflation and expanded federal investment returning to Nevada, their collective estimate is that Nevada will now lose $917 per person per year for every Nevadan missed in the 2010 Census. It is crucial to Nevada's allocation of federal funding from 2010-2020 that its response rate to the 2010 Census be maximized.

Start-Up Cost Estimate:	**$961,055**
Enhanced Savings/Revenue Estimates: 1-Year:	**$15,928,290**
5-Year:	**$79,641,450**

Explanation:
The 1990 Census was widely acknowledged to be unsuccessful in the State of Nevada. A limited national partnership program, combined with poor coordination with state and local governments, created antipathy toward the Census and precipitated a substantial undercount of the population. Nevada had the fifth-worst response rate in the nation in 1990 and the manner in which the Census was conducted was viewed as being out of touch with the state's political climate.

In 2000, the Interim Finance Committee of the Nevada State Legislature allocated $788,400 for a Nevada-oriented marketing and outreach program to supplement the national outreach campaign. The result of this investment was profound: Nevada had the best improvement in census response of any state in the nation. The undercount of Nevada's population, measured by the Census Bureau in 1990 to be 2.30% (sixth-worst in the country) was reduced significantly through this investment. An independent study by Price Waterhouse Coopers measured Nevada's 2000 undercount to be 1.68%, a substantial improvement. The start-up cost estimate, $961,055, is a comparable investment to the 2000 allocation, adjusted for inflation at 2%.

The 2000 state-specific marketing and outreach campaign, funded by the Interim Finance Committee, included advertising, mailed messaging to explain the benefits of participation, and Spanish-language outreach to select zip codes. The campaign repositioned the Census as being less of a federal mandate and more of a grassroots neighborhood campaign. This approach resonated with the public and substantially reduced the undercount.

The enhanced revenue estimates outlined above are based on the State Demographer's most recent estimate of Nevada's 2010 population: 2,801,551. Adopting a marketing and outreach strategy to keep the undercount at its 2000 level (1.68%) and avoiding a reversion to the 1990 level (2.30%) will result in the inclusion of 17,370 Nevadans in the official Census count. Given the $917 per person per year figure, the five year benefit to the state's economy amounts to over $79 million.

Recommendation #22

Reinstate the requirement that Proof of Insurance from a licensed Nevada   insurance company be presented to the Nevada Department of Motor Vehicles (DMV) for new vehicle registrations. Pursue programming on the DMV website to facilitate issuance of all temporary Proof of Insurance cards through the DMV website secure server.

Issue:

Nevada's uninsured driver rate is approximately 17-19%. Under previous leadership, DMV eliminated the requirement that proof of insurance cards must be presented for vehicle registrations. Reinstating the proof of insurance card requirement will help reduce the uninsured driver population by half, resulting in increased insurance premium tax revenues. DMV's current project of design and development of a web-based insurance verification program should include creating links with Nevada insurance companies and licensed agents to print proof of insurance cards from a secured DMV website.

Start-Up Cost Estimate:	**unknown**
Savings/Enhanced Revenue Estimates: 1 Year:	**$4.3 million**
5-Year:	**$21.5 million**

Explanation:

Nevada currently has 17-19% of its motorists driving uninsured motor vehicles. It is estimated that by cutting the uninsured population by half, the approximately 180,000 additional insured vehicles would generate $3.8 million annually in additional 3.5% insurance premium tax revenues and further protect Nevada citizens from the uninsured driver problem. The state will also realizes savings from reduced uninsured damage to state property and personal injuries paid out to innocent victims of uninsured accidents.

DMV is currently working with the insurance commissioner and industry representatives on design and development of a new web-based insurance verification program. This will replace the existing outdated and problematic system. As part of this effort, provisions could be made to incorporate issuance of all temporary "proof of insurance" cards from the DMV website, similar to what is now being done with smog checks and auto dealer reports of sale. This would give DMV and law enforcement immediate "proof of insurance," even if a registrant forgets to carry the "proof card" in the vehicle or bring it to DMV for registration. It would also eliminate the major part of fraudulent cards and phony insurance policies being sold by unauthorized agents and criminals, a problem experienced in Nevada for years. Although stronger criminal statutory language for this type of fraud was enacted, neither DMV, the Insurance Division nor the Attorney General has had the staff to pursue these crimes.

AB21, currently before the Legislature, addresses reinstatement of the proof of insurance card policy.

Recommendation #23

Bulk copies of Driver Instruction booklets should be provided at a cost of $2 per booklet. License applicants who return for additional drive tests beyond the second try should be charged a duplicate fee in recognition of the additional personnel and administrative time and costs.

Issue:
     Demand for printed copies of the Nevada Driver Education booklet has decreased significantly since the material was made available on the DMV website. However, of the approximately 200,000 copies still being printed each year, an estimated 92,000 are being supplied to schools in the state. These schools charge a fee for the instruction and should pay for the cost of the printed booklets. The incidence of repeat attempts to pass the drive test for licensing is significant, particularly for young drivers. Instituting a duplicate charge for this repeated use of the DMV personnel and time is appropriate.

Start-Up Cost Estimate: **None**
Savings/Enhanced Revenue Estimates: 1 Year: **$850,000**
                              5-Year: **$4.25 million**

Explanation:
     Although demand for printed Driver Instruction booklets has decreased, the state is still printing and distributing about 200,000 printed copies per year. Bulk quantities – an estimated 92,000 -- of these books are used by driver education schools that charge tuition for this instruction. Bulk copies (more than two) distributed to schools should be provided at a cost of $2 per booklet. DMV estimates the cost of printing the booklets is $1 per copy.
     A drive test is required of all young driver applicants and some adult applicants. DMV charges $21.25 for Instruction Permits for drivers under 65 and $16.25 for 65 and older Instruction Permits. No separate fee is charged for the drive test with a DMV technician. However, a meaningful number of drivers – some estimates run as high as 70% -- fail the drive test and must return for one or more additional drive tests. Instituting a duplicate fee for additional drive tests beyond the second try would help defray the personnel and operating costs. Assuming an incidence of 50% on the retry rate for the drive test, this is, at minimum, over 33,000 repeat uses of DMV personnel on under-65 applicants alone. In checking some other states around the country, it is more common than not to charge for each test, including the first, and driver permit fees are 25% to 55% higher.

Recommendation #24

The State should make statutory changes to the interest rates paid on overpayment of taxes and charged on underpayment of taxes for both individuals and businesses. The State should adopt the index used by the Internal Revenue Service, as adjusted periodically, for businesses and individuals.

Issue:

The State is currently paying 6% interest on tax overpayments it has received and is charging 12% interest on tax underpayments due to the State. This is in excess of interest rates charged and paid by the Federal government, banks and other states. There apparently exists no regular review and adjustment procedure for these rates by the State.

Start-Up Cost Estimate:	**Unknown**
Saving/Enhanced Revenue Estimates:1 Year:	**Unknown**
5 Year:	**Unknown**

Explanation:

The interest rates paid by the State to its taxpayers, both individuals and businesses, who are entitled to reimbursement for tax overpayments as well as the interest rate charged by the state for underpayment of taxes by individuals and businesses are currently in excess of rates paid and charged by the Federal government and in the private sector. The state currently has no statutory process in place to regularly review and adjust these rates. By aligning the rates charged and paid by the State with the Internal Revenue Service rates for businesses and individuals, the State's interest rates will be automatically adjusted in keeping with an agreed standard.

Recommendation #25

Nevada's Department of Information Technology (DoIT) should implement and maintain an Enterprise Web Content Management System capable of hosting agency Web content and Web based applications, providing a single point of access for Nevada's citizens, while reducing costs.

Issue:
Individual agency Web presence has created a redundancy of personnel tasks and increased costs. By acquiring a Web Content Management system, DoIT will be able to provide State agencies with a complete package supporting all of their needs with no additional charges to them. DoIT can then accommodate the approximately160 State-sponsored Web sites not currently being serviced by its Web Group, while maintaining its service to the 157 existing Web sites that are currently serviced by DoIT.

Start-Up Cost Estimate: **$76,500**
(Enterprise Web Content Management System software)
Savings/Enhanced Revenue Estimates: 1 Year   **$500,000**
                                 5 Year   **$1,500,000**
(Cumulative savings as all state agencies switch to DoIT)

Explanation:
DoIT currently supports 157 State agency Web sites. In order to properly support current customers and have the capability to accept new State customers, DoIT's Web Group needs to update current technology by acquiring a Web Content Management system.

The tool used currently by various Nevada agencies in Web development and maintenance is outdated and is no longer supportable. In order for them to achieve the necessary enhancements, they must be acquired outside DoIT's services. Accordingly, 500 new licenses for these services would need to be purchased at a cumulative State expense of $200,000, which does not include the cost of training to use the software. As the proposed DoIT Web Content Management system is an Enterprise system, there is no additional cost for individual licenses or any other software needed by using organizations.

Purchasing this Web Content Management system will provide the State with leading edge technology to build a much needed State portal with a consistent look and feel for all State sites. It will improve workflow, increase version control and approval authorization levels, provide better Web authorizing tools, help integrate Web services, promote Web site personalization and provide Web site consistency throughout State Web sites.

Recommendation #26

Establish a common email platform for all Executive Branch Agencies.

Issue:
When the UNR Center for Research and Design, a Nevada State entity, conducted a SAGE email survey of 17,000 State Executive Branch employees, it was able to reach only 13,777 of them after repeated attempts. One agency's email Spam protection prevented that entire agency from participating. Collaboration technologies link people, processes, and information within and across organization boundaries and are most effective when implemented using an enterprise approach. With multiple email systems, economies of scale, centralized collaboration, and functionality are lost, while hardware and software costs are excessive.

Start-Up Cost Estimate: **$6.49 per additional user per month**
Savings/Enhanced Revenue Estimates: 1 Year   **$150,000**
                                (based on adding 2,000 users each year)
                                5 Year   **$750,000**

Explanation:
Analysis indicates that regardless of the choice of email platform, the cost per user decreases as the user count grows. These economies of scale allow provision of additional services to user agencies without significant impacts on the overall cost of services. Through cooperative partnership with Nevada agencies, the Department of Information Technology is able to deploy value added services to the existing email environment such as:
— Common Address Books, which allow users to simply enter names rather than addresses when sending emails;
— Enhanced security through provision of the best anti-Spam and anti-Virus solutions available and by providing email service internally, rather than having an outside vendor house sensitive data;
— Shared calendaring and appointment scheduling, enabling users to schedule meetings without having to contact participants ahead of time; and,
— Provision of web access to every mailbox, enabling users to check email 24x7 from anywhere in the world.

Creation of collaboration systems based on broader, enterprise considerations is more likely to produce adaptive business solutions. Although point solutions for localized workgroup collaboration may provide improved user productivity, enhanced benefits can be realized through widespread integration into processes, workflow, and applications. Effective use of collaborative technologies provides a high degree of transparency by hiding the complexity of any underlying technologies in favor of accomplishing the business objective. Other services and enhancements possible in a common e-mail platform include:
— Centralized Scheduling of Resources
— Public Folders
— Fault Tolerant Mail Services
— Secure Wireless Email
— Instant Messaging / Audio/Video Conferencing & Collaboration possibilities

Recommendation #27
Nevada should significantly improve its State level energy conservation efforts by enforcing its existing energy conservation plan and revising that plan consistent with 2009 organizational, financial, statutory and technical realities.

Issue:
The Nevada Energy Conservation Plan for State Government was announced by the Governor in April, 2001. This plan tasked each agency of a department or a commission with writing, updating, and implementing an internal energy conservation plan. Several agencies were also assigned as coordinating agencies. No agencies received funding or manpower to implement or coordinate the plan. Agencies that were assigned monitoring responsibility did not provide monthly reports. Each department or commission was also asked to provide a semi-annual status report and an annual revision to their plan. Reports required under the Plan were not consistently provided, evaluated or centrally stored. Under 2009 NRS, the responsibility for energy conservation now rests with the Renewable Energy and Energy Efficiency Authority, Buildings and Grounds, Public Works Board, and the Purchasing Division. In FY2008, State buildings consumed 253.3 million KWH of electricity at a cost of over $25 million.

Start-Up Cost Estimate: Unknown
Savings/Enhanced Revenue Estimate: *Not available,*
but significant in other governments

Explanation:
To achieve significant savings through energy conservation efforts, Nevada State government should:

1. Revise, clarify and enforce its Energy Conservation Plan by incorporating new programs approved by the Governor and the 2009 Legislature and by resolving statutory duplications between NRS 331 and 701, as well as other NRS created by SB 358 and AB 522 of the 2009 Legislature.

2. Use federal energy conservation block grants under the Federal American Recovery and Reinvestment Act (ARRA) (stimulus funds) to seed sustainable programs and put in place long-term funding mechanisms such as revolving loans and energy savings performance contracting. Nevada expects to receive $34.7 million in such funds in four installments and proposes to use $7 million of that for energy efficiency retrofits of State buildings, working with NV Energy under various DOE restrictions. AB 522 was enacted and authorizes creation of an ARRA revolving loan fund for renewable energy, energy efficiency and energy conservation.

3. Take full advantage of the State Board of Examiners approved contract with LPB Energy Consulting to cut utility bills and potentially save $6 million by 2013. LPB will capture and analyze utility data, helping State agencies reduce total energy cost and consumption. NDOT, Buildings and Grounds and Department of Military will participate in an initial pilot program.

4. Apply for NV Energy Fort Churchill Generating Area (Carson City) Sure Bet commercial retrofit projects through December, 2009, and other Sure Bet incentives to maximize acquisition and use of remote mounted occupancy sensors in existing facilities and in capital improvement projects.

5. Consider immediate savings opportunities like turning State computers off completely when they are not in use. Other governments and private sector businesses are achieving major savings in this way.

Recommendation #28

Request appointment of an Interim Legislative Committee to study the Public Works process.

Issue:
The complexity and costs of the Public Works process are enormous. This process is criticized by most outsiders as causing capital projects in Nevada to cost far more and to take much longer to complete than necessary.

Start-Up Cost Estimate: **Unavailable**
Savings/Enhanced Revenue Estimate: **Unavailable**

Explanation:
    Although they are routinely and energetically defended by Public Works Board insiders, most other Nevadans familiar with the building industry believe that Nevada's capital construction process is counter-productive in a variety of ways. Only a thorough study by legislators, who can then take necessary corrective action, is likely to resolve these differences of opinion.

Recommendation #29

Nevada Revised Statute (NRS) 408 regarding design-build contracts should be expanded to allow both an increased number of such projects per year and a significantly lower dollar threshold limit on such contracts.

Issue:
The existing NRS is both unclear and overly restrictive regarding design/build contracts. Such restrictions and lack of clarity prevent the State from taking full advantage of the cost effectiveness of such contracts for certain construction projects.

Start-Up Cost Estimate:	**Unknown**
Savings/Enhanced Revenue Estimate:	**Unknown**

Explanation:
NRS 408.388 states, under subsection 2: "once each fiscal year, contract with a design-build team."

The attorney General's office has interpreted this language to restrict such contracts to one per year. The NRS also requires that the estimated cost of the design-build project must exceed $20 million, along with certain other restrictions. This language needs to be expanded to raise the number of contracts allowed. NDOT and others recommend that the dollar threshold be lowered significantly. All such contracts would have to meet other NRS qualifications for a project. None of these changes is intended to prevent smaller contractors and teams from bidding on any NDOT or other State contract under design-bid-build processes or to restrict their participation in design-build team bidding.

Recommendation #30

In connection with SAGE Commission Recommendation #18 — review of costs and fees — included in the December 31, 2008 Report to the Governor, the following definitions should be adopted.

Fee: A charge made to recover the cost of operating the program or providing the service, including indirect cost (overhead). A fee shall not be used for any purpose other than the actual direct and indirect cost of the program or service being provided to the end user.

Cost: Direct cost of the program or service plus its allocable portion of indirect cost. Direct costs are those that can be identified specifically with a particular final cost objective. Indirect costs are those: (a) incurred for a joint or common purpose benefitting more than one cost objective; and (b) not readily assignable to the cost objectives specifically benefitted without effort disproportionate to the results achieved. (*from OMB Circular A-87*)

<u>Issue:</u>
When fees are set for a particular product or service, it is important that a consistent approach be taken in arriving at the amount of the fee.

Start-Up Cost Estimate: **None Identified**
Savings/Enhanced Revenue Estimate: **Unknown**

<u>Explanation:</u>
These definitions will ensure that the same methodology is used to establish the amount of fees, both between the various departments of state government, and over a succession of years.

Recommendation #31

Authorize the Department of Corrections (DOC) to establish an intermediate sanction facility for certain probation violators and offenders, who are determined to be substance abusers. Substance abuse treatment is to be provided by the Department of Health and Human Services (HHS).

Issue:
The cost of incarceration in Nevada prisons is approximately $22,000 per year per inmate. Alternative sentencing programs and specialty courts in Nevada communities have proven to be most successful in keeping certain non-violent offenders out of its expensive prison system.

Start-Up Cost Estimate:	**$6 million**
Enhanced Savings/Revenue Estimates: 1-Year:	**$51.2 million**
5-Year:	**$280 million**

Explanation:
This recommendation, initially proposed as Senate Bill 398 in the 2009 Legislative Session, would establish intermediate sanction and detention facilities to provide treatment for substance abuse issues under court order. It would be used for alternative sentenced offenders, probation and selected parole violators. Substance abuse treatment would be provided by HHS, while offenders were under DOC control. Treatment and detention costs would be borne by the offenders to the extent they are able to pay. Courts could order community service for those determined to be unable to pay. Upon successful completion of mandated treatment and other court orders, courts could set aside the conviction of an offender or return a probation or parole violator to probation or parole. DOC will implement a pilot program from existing resources initially modeled on Hawaii "Hope Courts" to determine how such facilities should be administered and operated.

Among issues to be evaluated in the pilot program are actual costs, levels of patient control, recidivism rates, treatment options and time lines. Depending on levels of patient control ordered by the courts and the health status of each individual involved, federal Medicaid dollars could be leveraged to provide some of this treatment.

Cost estimates for this recommendation are based on existing annual estimates of alternative sentence adjudications and probation violators along with recidivism rates for these types of offenders. The pilot program will establish more accurate cost and savings estimates.

Three sworn Washoe County Sheriff Alternative Sentencing Supervisory Officers and a single Case Manager currently monitor 400 offenders there. Clark County currently has Alternative Sentencing programs only in certain judicial districts. Follow-on treatment mandated by the court is, therefore, sporadic and difficult for offenders, supervisory officers and treatment providers. The District Courts, parole and probation authorities have little ability to transition, lodge or sanction violators. An interim sanction facility could provide a viable treatment option for these probationers, parole violators and other offenders.

Recommendation #32

**Nevada's information technology future should be defined through
a comprehensive strategic planning process organized and developed by the State Information Technology Advisory Board (ITAB).
Implementation of the resulting plan should be monitored, measured, and evaluated by a project manager separate from ITAB and
the Department of Information Technology (DoIT).**

Issue:
Nevada's information technology infrastructure, enterprise architecture, and
facilities have been allowed to evolve over many years absent any overarching
planning process. Centralization of key elements, like a common email platform and an enterprise web content management system, is being implemented without reference to any broader strategic objective than centralization itself.

Start-Up Cost Estimate:	**Unavailable**
Savings/Enhanced Revenue Estimate:	**Unavailable**

Explanation:
The ITAB reports to the Governor and is supposed to meet quarterly. It has
not met in two years. It should be reconstituted for the specific purpose of
creating, in coordination with strategic planners in the Department of Administration, a cost effective Information Technology Strategic Plan for Nevada. This process should include, but not be limited to:

A Vision of Nevada's Future (2020-2025)
Nevada's Strategic Goals
DoIT's Strategic Goals

- Enable the State to focus on its business because information technology is as ubiquitous as electricity.

- Provide customized, integrated, full-service online government to all Nevada citizens.

- Develop and maintain the technology to help Nevada businesses to grow along with its population.

- Know how technology is being used for Nevada and maintain transparency about such use.

- Become a conduit among all information assets to promote, leverage and value-add sharing.

DoIT's Objectives

DoIT's Initiatives

DoIT Technical Model

DoIT Data Models

Recommendation #33

Change the Interim Finance Committee (IFC) oversight thresholds as follows:

A) Whenever a request for the revision of a work program of a department, institution or agency in an amount more than $50,000 would, when considered with all other changes in allotments for that work program, increase or decrease by 10 percent or $110,00, whichever is less, the expenditure level approved by the legislature. (NRS 353.220.4)

B) For gifts and non-governmental grants exceeding $25,000 each and governmental grants exceeding $225,000 each and any grant that involves new employees. (NRS 353.335.5a and 5b)

C) Specifically exclude revision of work program requests for balance forward funds and/ or authority to the subsequent fiscal year where legislative authority exists and with no change in purpose; and de-augmentation of expenditure authority from any additional IFC approvals. (NRS 353.220.5 ADD 5d), d(i) and d(ii))

D) The legislature shall review and adjust these amounts every six years. (NRS 353.220.5 ADD 5e)

Issue:
In open-ended responses to a survey conducted by the SAGE Commission, State employees uniformly criticized the IFC process as politicized and expensive. The investment of human resources required to apply for changes at the existing thresholds, set over 10 years ago, is out of proportion to amount of the requested changes. In order to cut down on this waste, they recommended raising the IFC oversight threshold to levels more relative to the dollar amounts of current budget totals and government and non-government grants. Former State Budget Directors have made the same recommendation.

Start-Up Cost Estimate: **Unavailable**
Savings/Enhanced Revenue Estimate: **Unavailable**

Explanation:
Work program changes and acceptance of grants and gifts must first be approved by the Governor.

In addition, existing NRS require that work program changes and acceptance of gifts and grants be submitted to the IFC for advance approval at the following thresholds:

--- Whenever a request for the revision of a work program of a department, institution or agency in an amount more than $20,000 would, when considered with all other changes in allotments for that work program increase or decrease by 10 percent or $50,000.

--- For gifts and grants from nongovernmental sources, not to exceed $10,000 and governmental grants not exceeding $100,000 each in value.

These thresholds were established over ten years ago and have not been adjusted for inflation or current fiscal realities.

The new threshold levels in this recommendation were calculated by applying population growth and CPI factors to the amounts set by the Legislature in 1997, as found in the provision that limits Budget growth.

Recommendation #34

Revise language in NRS 242.131 so that State agencies, boards, and commissions in the Executive Department are not exempt from using Nevada Department of Information Technology (DoIT) professional services except for those infrastructures, enterprise architectures, facilities and personnel required for control of the specialized mission of the enterprise.

<u>Issue:</u>
By allowing blanket exemptions, a proliferation of enterprise services has been designed, built, and deployed throughout the State. Agencies have created competing infrastructures and sourced enterprise services unrelated to their specialized missions, creating unnecessary expenses to the State that would have been avoided by using existing DoIT-provided services or solutions.

Start-Up Cost Estimate: **Not Available**

Savings/Enhanced Revenue Estimates:
Savings would be derived from the removal of redundant systems, including duplicate hardware, software and IT staffing assigned to these duties at the applicable agency, board or commission, which are not unique to the mission requirements of that specific enterprise. Estimates would be determined by the agency, board or commission affected, based on the level of duplication which would be avoided through support provided by the DoIT.

<u>Explanation:</u>
One of the many mandates for the Department of Information Technology as described in NRS 242.071 is *"to prevent the unnecessary proliferation of equipment and personnel among the various state agencies."* This proposal is designed to accomplish that goal by removing exemptions in NRS 242.131 from DoIT-provided services which are neither unique to nor required by the mission of the agency, board or commission involved. This change will eliminate the proliferation and duplication of IT equipment and personnel that currently exist in various state agencies, boards, and commissions across State Government for purposes which are not unique to the enterprise involved.

DoIT would be responsible for collaborating with all State agencies, boards, and commissions to eliminate redundant or duplicate enterprise services or solutions, eliminating waste and reducing overall State expenses, while allowing these entities to maintain control over infrastructures, enterprise architectures, facilities and personnel critical to accomplishment of the unique mission of that agency, board or commission.

Recommendation #35

Solicit recommendations for a common telecommunications platform for all Executive branch State agencies and invite the Judicial and Legislative branches, Constitutional Officers, the Nevada System of Higher Education (NSHE), and cities and counties throughout the State to participate.

Issue:

Currently, each State agency uniquely supports and maintains individual telecommunication systems. The State could realize significant savings in operations, maintenance and support by further expanding the use of its existing voice over internet protocol (VoIP) fiber backbone, by employing open source VoIP solutions or by outsourcing to an external vendor.

Start-Up Cost Estimate:	**Unavailable**
Savings/Enhanced Revenue Estimates:	**Unavailable**

Explanation:

With each State agency responsible for purchasing, maintaining, and supporting its individual telecommunication systems, economies of scale are lost, increasing overall State expenditures. Analysis indicates that the cost per user decreases as the total user count grows with economies of scale. Through cooperative partnerships with Nevada agencies, the Department of Information Technology (DoIT) has reduced telecommunication costs by deploying a common VoIP fiber backbone that most agencies are using. However, more extensive use of this backbone by State agencies will reduce overall State telecommunication systems costs.

One possibility is outsourcing these systems to an external vendor. Outsourcing has the potential to enhance the user experience with more support for current and future technologies like Unified Communications (UC) and VoIP while further reducing overall State expenses. UC is the ability to integrate communications and collaboration in a rich, multimedia experience that can include unified telephony, voice, video, telecommuting, instant messaging, web conferencing, e-mail, voice mail, whiteboards, and business applications, allowing for increased employee productivity. There also exists a wide variety of other VoIP options which should be considered, including open source VoIP solutions.

The State should proceed with a request for information (RFI) to outline the best solution(s) and follow up with a request for proposals (RFP) to determine and compare the implementation costs and overall long-term savings to the State of the various options available. Other government entities that have migrated to VoIP technology have engaged outside vendors to prepare RFI and RFP.

Recommendation #36

Explore the possibility of an exchange of Ely State Prison and Lovelock Correctional Center to companies that specialize in private corrections in return for construction of similar facilities located within existing large population centers to be determined by the Board of Prison Commissioners.

<u>Issue:</u>
Currently, Ely State Prison and Lovelock Correctional Center are located in rural areas of the State which results in much higher operational costs than the other major corrections facilities in Nevada. While abandonment of these existing facilities could prove to be an economic hardship for the communities and the staff involved, their exchange would guarantee ongoing economic benefits to the rural communities, while simultaneously allowing the State to reduce Department of Corrections (DOC) operational costs and to provide more efficient and effective facilities.

Start-Up Cost Estimate: **None Identified**
Savings/Enhanced Revenue Estimate: No estimates available at this time.

<u>Explanation:</u>
　　Nevada experiences significantly higher Department of Corrections operational costs in the rural communities of Ely and Lovelock. There are inadequate hospitals in the communities and the offenders are far away from the courts that will evaluate their appeals and petitions. Thus, medical care, legal costs, transportation and personnel costs are higher than similarly sized facilities located near the major population centers. Additionally, the Department experiences a "boom, bust" cycle of employment, depending on how well the mining industry is doing in those rural locations. Consequently, there are greater costs associated with commuting, overtime and staffing of vacant positions. In addition, visiting opportunities are lower and there is a great amount of literature that suggests family support and ongoing ties reduce future recidivism.

　　This proposal it to explore the possibility that private correctional companies might be interested in obtaining these prisons in Nevada. In exchange, Nevada would request that the private company construct similar prison space in more centralized locations in the State that would be more cost effective for the DOC. Private companies have demonstrated an ability to construct facilities more rapidly, at lower costs while using the latest technology. In addition to the simple exchange, it is recommended that if such an agreement could be reached, Nevada would have the first right of refusal for any available private bed space should any unexpected DOC population crisis occur, which has happened before.

　　There are a number of advantages to a private company that further support this course of action. Privatization of prisons continues to expand in the United States and this proposal could result in an economic diversion that would benefit both State government as well as the rural communities in question. This proposal could also allow the State to modernize facilities at minimal or no cost to the General Fund.

Recommendation #37

The Department of Corrections (DOC) should issue a request for proposals (RFP) to evaluate the costs and benefits of privatization of inmate medical and mental health care and the provision of pharmaceutical services.

Issue:
The cost of incarceration is in Nevada prisons is approximately $22,000 per year per inmate. One of the largest components of that inmate cost is providing medical care. DOC is responsible for investigating alternatives to provide a sufficient minimal level of inmate care to meet constitutional standards at a reduced cost to the State.

Start-Up Cost Estimate:	**$25,000**
Savings/Enhanced Revenue Estimates:1 Year	**$4.5 million**
5 Year	**$24.1 million**

Explanation:
In 1995, DOC privatized medical/mental health care at the Ely State Prison and Conservation Camp, which represented 15% of the total inmate population in Nevada. This privatized care was provided at a lower per inmate cost than for the rest of the system. During the period 1995-2000, prison medical care costs were reduced at Ely while no litigation costs for the State were incurred there. Currently, Clark and Washoe Counties, Las Vegas, North Las Vegas and Henderson outsource private medical care for their jails from four different providers. Prison medical care should involve economies of scale, since the Nevada prison system is so much larger than these county and city jails.

Nineteen states have entirely privatized inmate health care, with the two largest providers currently serving over 375 sites and 350,000 inmates. These companies indemnify their state clients for all litigation and losses. This does not mean that there will be no litigation naming the state or its DOC. It means that the contracted company will defend such suits and pay the prevailing party for any losses incurred. There are currently significant litigations involving Nevada DOC medical care, exposing the State to over a million dollars in losses and possible mandates for care from federal courts.

Medical cost containment is critical in every medical delivery system, but it is particularly important in corrections. In the face of dwindling resources, Nevada has the following choices: 1) continue to run the operation itself; 2) Develop a relationship with other public services like the State Department of Health and Human Services (DHHS) to run the system for DOC; 3) contract with a private company that has particular experience in correctional healthcare; 4) allow existing State employees to match private provider contract terms.

Recommendation #37, *continued*

Explanation, *continued from previous page*

This proposal is for the DOC to issue an RFP or an RFI to compare these three choices so that a rational and cost effective method of health care delivery can be selected. Some of the benefits to look for in the comparison of costs between private medical and government operated medical are: 1) an immediate reduction in State personnel costs; 2) a reduction in the future liability of the PERS retirement system; 3) an immediate reduction in the State cost for PEBP benefits; 4) a reduction in personnel supervision workload by the agency; 5) a reduction in the cost of litigation for the DOC and the Attorney General, as well as reductions in the legal liability exposure to staff; 6) a reduction in the cost of contract nurses; 7) a reduction in the cost of pharmaceutical expenses; 8) an increase in the professional experience in the medical staff on site; 9) an increased level of care to inmates at a reduced cost; 10) Accreditations from the American Correctional Association and the National Commission on Correctional Health Care at no cost to the State, which are not currently awarded under the State operated system.

The State is not bound to accept a bid based on any RFI or RFP, but the information provided should be ready for inclusion in 2011 DOC medical budget preparations.

Recommendation #38

Require directors of cabinet level departments to establish and implement cross training programs for their employees where feasible and practical, within a reasonable time. The goals of any such program should be to 1) help meet peak workloads and improve operational efficiency; 2) offer job enrichment opportunities; and 3) reduce costs by reducing use of outside contracts and/or overtime.

<u>Issue:</u>
Open-ended responses to the SAGE survey of State employees indicated a widespread desire to participate in cross training programs. With budget and other fiscal constraints requiring employee furloughs and increasing use of alternative work schedules, management at all levels has considerable incentive to accommodate this desire.

Start-Up Cost Estimate: **Unknown**
Savings/Enhanced Revenue Estimate: **Unknown**

<u>Explanation:</u>
Cross training is integral to effective succession planning and allows others to fill in when someone is ill or on vacation and during peak workload periods. Cross training is occurring in a sporadic, informal manner across State government thanks to the initiative and professionalism of State employees. It should be formalized.

There is no cookie cutter approach to cross training since it often is peculiar to the specific functional area or job involved. Each department director should be encouraged to adapt cross training programs which do not violate existing job description or classification restrictions to the nature of the work or services provided by the subordinate work units of the department involved.

Discussions with certain agency directors indicate that there are opportunities both within and between departments for cross training. Potential interagency cross training opportunities include the eligibility staffs in Health and Human Services (DHHS) and in the Employment Security Division of the Department of Employment Training and Rehabilitation (DETR), as well as collaboration between the Department of Transportation's Right of Way staff and personnel in the divisions of State Lands and Water Resources of the Department of Conservation and Natural Resources.

These discussions also identified a number of obstacles to cross training. These include restrictions on "out of class" work (16 hours) without compensation, the current employee evaluation system, the current position control number system, and the lack of communication and coordination of sharing opportunities within and between departments. These obstacles should be addressed and mitigated where possible.

Recommendation #39

The Nevada Department of Transportation (NDOT) should perform a detailed analysis and review of all of the existing NDOT maintenance stations throughout the State with a view to eliminating some stations and consolidating others.

<u>Issue:</u>
There are 45 NDOT maintenance stations across the State, an average of one every 56 miles along Interstate 80 and US Highways 50 and 95. Most of these stations were established before these roads became the modern systems they are today. There are thirty-five rural maintenance stations with only six of these employing over eight persons each. Just to maintain these smaller stations costs an average of $63,000 per year, not counting salaries and benefits.

Start-Up Cost Estimate:	**$100,000**
Savings/Enhanced Revenue Estimates: 1 Year	**$650,000**
5 Year	**$4,400,000**

<u>Explanation:</u>
This proposal envisions that a study of existing maintenance stations statewide would allow for the elimination or consolidation of at least twenty-five percent of the smaller, rural stations. Maintenance budgets in most states have been cut. Although states are attempting to maintain adequate response times for weather-related road maintenance issues, particularly snow removal, they are also trying to do so with fewer employees. They are also dropping levels of service in aesthetic areas of service like litter removal and mowing.

NDOT needs to review its rural area road maintenance practices, particularly the placement and manning of maintenance stations in view of ongoing fiscal realities, the enhanced capabilities of the equipment used, the nature of the roadways being maintained and the seasonal nature of the need for smaller, outlying stations. Perhaps temporary seasonal maintenance outposts could be created using equipment and personnel from the larger remaining stations whose mowing and litter removal requirements would be curtailed during the winter months, anyway.

Recommendation #40

The Nevada Department of Transportation (NDOT) should commission a study of the costs and benefits associated with providing roadway maintenance by NDOT maintenance crews compared to outsourcing the same maintenance activities and develop decision factors for outsourcing such maintenance.

Issue:

NDOT currently owns large amounts of construction equipment to accomplish roadway maintenance which it has historically performed. In order to amortize the costs of owning and maintaining this equipment inventory and because it allows the Department to perform other construction and maintenance tasks at nominally lower costs, it seeks to put available equipment and personnel to work on projects which could be cost effectively outsourced. Such outsourcing would allow NDOT to reduce its equipment inventory and some personnel, thereby saving the costs of acquiring and maintaining unnecessary equipment along with significant personnel expenses.

Start-Up Cost Estimate: **Not available**
Savings/Enhanced Revenue Estimates: **Not available**

Explanation:

NDOT owns and maintains thousands of pieces of equipment. It has 1464 small vehicles and trucks for 1750 employees. It owns large motor graders, medium to large dozers, grinders, milling machines, distributor trucks, radial stackers and conveyers, all of which are more associated with road construction than with road maintenance. This proposal is to help NDOT develop decision factors for determining whether and when to outsource maintenance projects which would allow it to divest itself of large amounts of this expensive and problematic equipment. It seeks to allow NDOT to avoid costly competition with Nevada's large, diverse and cost effective private sector road construction industry.

Some of the decision factors such a study should address are:

- emergency and immediate maintenance responses, like snow removal.
- short term repairs of limited scope like damaged guard rails, potholes and drainage.
- large scale rehabilitations like chip sealing, or large scale contracts like district wide culvert cleaning.
- paving and striping where contractors generally have equipment and expertise.
- contractor availability, depending on the geographic area involved and mobilization requirements.
- time sensitivity. Except for emergencies, NDOT contracts take 6-9 months to develop, timelines which should be thoroughly analyzed in any study.
- cost factors.

Recommendation #41

Create a communication structure, managed by a Nevada State Grants Coordinator, to facilitate dissemination of grant application opportunities and collaborative application efforts between agencies, county and local governments and non-profits, and identify a resource pool of experts and grant writers to support agencies in preparing applications. Create Grant Writer positions in selected state departments based on availability of grant opportunities.

Issue:

On a per capita basis by Federal Agency, Nevada is ranked 50th in the U.S. Census Bureau report on *Federal Aid to States for Fiscal Year 2008*. Another Census report shows Nevada's per capita return on each federal tax dollar, as a percent of U.S. per capita levels, at .75 compared with .95 for states in the West Region. For grants alone, Nevada's return is .65 compared with 1.06 for the West Region. To ensure that Nevada is getting its share of federal funding, the state should create a structure to assist personnel in various agencies in this process. Currently, a significant number of opportunities for federal funding are not pursued because of inadequate availability of grants writers and a lack of communication structure among state agencies and with county, local and non-profit entities. The creation of a communication structure, the addition of a state Grants Coordinator and as many as four grant writer positions will strengthen the state's ability to pursue funding and increase the ability of agencies to partner with each other and with outside entities. The return on this investment is estimated at a 3% increase in federal grant funding in year one and a 10% increase by year five.

Start-Up Cost Estimate: **$450,000**
Savings/Enhanced Revenue Estimates: 1-Year: **$93 million**
                                              5-Year: **$310 million**

Explanation:

The key to success of central Grants offices in other states is communication. This works in three ways: 1) Having designated personnel who track and distribute information on funding opportunities that match state programs; 2) Coordinating application efforts among state departments, agencies, and non-profit organizations; 3) Developing and maintaining communication channels for personnel in the state who are responsible for writing applications.

The communication structure to be developed would include the following: 1) Creation of a State Grants Coordinator position, likely in the Budget Office; 2) Each state department, agency and division designates a key contact for grant information and establishes a communication network to the key contact within the agency; 3) A resource pool of existing and retired state workers is identified for subject-specific consultation and assistance with grant applications; 4) A public grants information website listing contacts, resources, grants that have been awarded to the state, grant opportunity notifications, and research data links; 5) Grant Writer positions should be added in the Department of Human Services and other state departments based on availability of grant opportunities; 6) Master Service Agreements (MSAs) should be established with outside grant writing contractors for access by agencies on a needs basis with a fund established for payments; 7) Agreements with Nevada's Higher Education System should be established to provide grant writer interns to state agencies; 8) Opportunities for free training from federal entities should be pursued; 9) Interim Finance Committee thresholds for accepting governmental grants should be raised, per SAGE Commission Recommendation #33.

Recommendation 42

Undertake a pilot project at one or more agencies to implement changes in Nevada's budget system. The pilot project should present, in the agencies selected, a program budget with clear performance evaluation criteria. The program budget should include funding in broad expenditure categories, as opposed to the three-part line item objects of expenditure, and measurable expected results at that level of funding should be included. The program budget can be presented with, or instead of, the traditional line item budget.

Issue:
Nevada's current budget system is flawed in several important respects: 1) The incremental funding approach (base + maintenance + enhancements) offers no practical way within a short legislative session to critically review basic expenditures. The majority of the time is spent considering add-ons. 2) The performance measures included are, for the most part, ignored for purposes of making funding decisions. 3) Line item budgeting focuses attention on the details of the budget instead of the anticipated results of the program

Start-up Cost Estimate: **Unknown**
                                               (minimal)

Savings/Enhanced Revenue Projection: **None**
                                    (will improve effectiveness)

Explanation:
A program budget would be structured in a results-oriented way with funding based on tasks to be accomplished provided in flexible categories instead of inflexible, object-of-expenditure line items. Performance evaluation criteria must be developed for all programs.

Budgeting decisions would be based on a review of performance evaluation data from the previous budget cycle instead of just starting with the last cycle's budget and adding on for increased workload, inflation, etc. The "base" budget would be subject to a review each cycle at the program level, not the line item or category level.

Recommendation #43

**A method of establishing budget funding priorities based on differ-
ent levels of expected revenues, should be adopted.**

Issue:
Lack of funding priorities developed during the construction of the budget
leads to across-the-board type cuts when revenues come in below forecasts.
This results in critical programs being reduced to the same extent as non-
critical programs. Reductions in critical programs may become necessary
eventually but non-critical programs should be reduced or eliminated first.

Start-Up Cost Estimate: **Unknown (minimal)**
Savings/Enhanced Revenue Estimate   **None (directly)**

Explanation:
Priority funding budgeting would require the Governor and then the Legislature to establish program funding priorities each budget cycle. The priorities would be grouped into broad bands (or "buckets"), for example, A, B and
C. Band A priorities would include critical services that should be funded if at
all possible. Band B would include services that the Governor and Legislature
would like to fund if revenues are available. Band C would include programs
to be funded if revenues exceed expectations.

The State must collect enough revenue to fund all programs in Band A
before Band B can be funded. All of Band B must be funded before the Band
C items. Since the A Band is a conservative level of funding, it has a very
high chance of being reached. The B Band has a lesser chance, and so on,
with the last Band usually not being funded unless the economy well outper-
forms forecasts.

This process allows priority setting each biennium and provides an orderly
process for cutting if the economy experiences a downturn. The State of
Arkansas has successfully used such a priority funding system since 1945.

Recommendation #44

Increase efforts to reduce costs for prescription drugs in the departments of Health and Human Services and Corrections by continuing ongoing programs and investigating new initiatives.

Issue:

The State of Nevada spends over $126 million per year on prescription drugs through its Medicaid, Mental Health, Corrections and other programs. The costs of these drugs have increased historically at a rate significantly higher than inflation. If these costs could be better controlled then significant savings could be realized.

Start-up Cost Estimate: **Unknown**
Savings/Enhanced Revenue Projection: **1 Year $5.1 million***
                                                                               5 Year $27.8 million*

*Based on increased usage, to 50%, of generic anti-psychotic drugs only.
Estimates are not possible on other elements of this proposal.

Explanation:

Reductions in drug costs are possible by pursuing initiatives in several areas as indicated below:

1) Continue efforts by Department of Health and Human Services to qualify for special pricing available under The 340B Drug Pricing Program of Public Law 102-585, the Veterans Health Care Act of 1992. Indications are that Medicaid, Mental Health, and Corrections are excluded from this pricing. However, mental health patients, and perhaps others, may become eligible through federally qualified health centers.

2) Expand efforts, including review of NRS restrictions, to maximize use of generic drugs. The percent of generic drugs used is very high for most kinds of drugs. The exceptions are anti-psychotic and some anti-depressants. Since the cost of generics can be 20% to 40% of the cost of brand name drugs, efforts should be made to use generics where appropriate.

3) Although State Purchasing has been able to hold down Nevada's costs with very advantageous pricing it obtained through a multi-state purchasing consortium, the other consortia in existence, and there are several, should be reviewed periodically to ensure best pricing.

4) Ensure that both quantity and dosage limits are in place to minimize waste.

5) Investigate the effect on drugs costs overall if other governmental entities within the state such as public hospitals and the Public Employee Benefits Program combined their purchasing power with the state.

6) Ensure that care coordination (case management and prescription management) is maximized to increase effectiveness of treatment and minimize waste.

Made in the USA
Charleston, SC
25 February 2010